P9-AEX-357

The Reconstruction of Lisbon

The Reconstruction of Lisbon

Severa's Legacy and the Fado's Rewriting of Urban History

Michael Colvin

Lewisburg
Bucknell University Press

Associated University Presses
2010 Eastpark Boulevard
Cranbury, NJ 08512

The paper used in this publication meets the requirements of the American National Standard for Permanence of Paper for Printed Library Materials Z39.48-1984.

Library of Congress Cataloging-in-Publication Data

Colvin, Michael, 1970–
The Reconstruction of Lisbon : Severa's legacy and the Fado's rewriting of urban history / Michael Colvin.
p. cm.
Includes bibliographical references and index.
ISBN 978-0-8387-5708-6 (alk. paper)
1. Fados—Portugal—Lisbon—History and criticism. 2. Severa, Maria, 1820–1846. 3. Mouraria (Lisbon, Portugal)—History. 4. Dantas, Júlio, 1876–1962. Severa. I. Title.
ML3718.F3C66 2008
946.9′42—dc22 2007051294

PRINTED IN THE UNITED STATES OF AMERICA

To my best friend, Dan Wilbur, who was with me the first time that I saw the Mouraria. By your third visit to Lisbon you appreciated the city's whorish charms, and now you sing her praises. And to Saag Alu, who has gotten closer to Lisbon's streets than I, and who behaves like such a ruffian that the locals have nicknamed him *Fera.*

Contents

Preface: The Mouraria at Face Value

It's not easy to place the ancient and the modern side by side.
—António de Oliveira Salazar

MY FIRST TRIP TO THE MOURARIA WAS ALSO MY FIRST TRIP TO LISBON and to Europe. I was a twenty-three-year-old graduate student who had a vague notion of Portuguese urban topography, distorted by the busy, and at times, kitschy aesthetics of the Portuguese immigrant enclaves of Newark, New Jersey, and Philadelphia. I was traveling with a friend who, like most Americans who visit Europe for the first time, would have preferred to see Paris or London. Our expectations of a European capital—mine fed by Newark's Ferry Street or Philadelphia's Rising Sun Avenue, and my friend's by the degraded images of Place Vendôme and Picadilly Circus in Hollywood movies—were thwarted when, on the second day of our journey, I decided that we would find the Castelo de São Jorge on foot. How hard could it be? You could see the reconstructed medieval castle walls and towers looming on the hill from everywhere in Lisbon.

I told the innkeeper at the small hotel on Avenida da Liberdade that, on our way to the castle, we would explore the Mouraria—a toponym that echoed in my head from a popular march on a Fado record:

Mouraria garrida, muito presumida, muito requebrada
Tem seu todo galdério
Seu ar de mistério
De moira encantada.[1]

[Vibrant, pretentious, languid Mouraria
Has its whorish charms
The mysterious ways
Of a bewitched Moorish girl.]

She reacted by warning me of the dangers of the neighborhood. My friend, who did not understand Portuguese, saw only the innkeeper's exaggerated gesture of doom as she motioned with her fingers a razor slitting her throat. However, I dismissed the old woman's caution because I had to see the Mouraria for myself. What little I had heard of Lisbon's riverside was from the Fado, and in the Fado, the Mouraria seemed worth the risk. Besides, I had been to many places in my own city where I might have been murdered, yet none of them had made their way into a popular song.

My friend and I followed a simple route to the Mouraria: from Praça dos Restauradores, we descended the Travessa de Santo Antão, turned right on Rua das Portas de Santo Antão, past the Ginjinha pubs on Largo de São Domingos, left on Rua de Barros Queirós, and a sharp left on Rua da Palma, where we stumbled upon the apparent aftermath of disaster. The charming, yet decadent eighteenth- and nineteenth-century Lisbon had come to a screeching halt. Before us lay a wasteland: Largo de Martim Moniz before the 1998 Expo when the city installed fountains and benches in the area that perpetually would be known as *o buraco* [the hole]. To our right, we spied a row of deteriorated seventeenth- and eighteenth-century houses, interrupted by the concrete and steel Centro Comercial Martim Moniz: an imitation, perhaps, of the most unimaginative American urban architecture of the 1980s. Straight ahead, beyond the tragic void in the city landscape, I could see more pre-Republican houses, divided by a thoroughfare: Avenida do Almirante Reis, similar to Avenida da Liberdade, yet without the fanfare and allusions to Lisbon's glorious history. The hideous Centro Comercial Martim Moniz's uglier twin, the Centro Comercial Mouraria, seemed clumsy, towering over two- and three-story buildings with plaster and tile façades.

Martim Moniz, pilgrim martyr of the 1147 Lisbon Siege, was crushed in a gate on the Moors' castle bluffs when he tried to gain entry into Islamic Lixbuna for the Portuguese and Anglo-Norman soldiers. Lisbon has commemorated the crusader's sacrifice by putting his name on the bloodied gate at the Castelo de São Jorge; on the subway station underneath the Baixa Mouraria—decorated with caricatures of the medieval warrior—; and on a plaza that until 1998 constituted the most cadaverous hiatus in the capital's architectural continuity.[2]

"A nightmare could begin here," urban historian Marina Tavares Dias comments on the hostile trench of the Baixa Mouraria.[3] Indeed, some of Lisbon's nightmares do begin here! Largo de Martim Moniz and the adjacent neighborhoods of Intendente and Anjos have absorbed the drug addicts and dealers who were displaced in the demolition of Lisbon's most infamous shantytown, Casal Ventoso. I have seen, on occasion, the unfortunate zombies of that nightmare walking on Avenida do Almirante Reis, a zone that is not recommended for the faint-of-heart tourist. My friend who lives on Rua de Angola, in Anjos, regularly urges me to take the subway or a taxi to bypass the Avenue and streets between his house and the Mouraria. And a French expatriate friend who was living in the bourgeois Campo de Ourique neighborhood told me, "I don't go there," as he grew tense at my mention of the Mouraria, "I was mugged there at knifepoint."

Just when my friend and I thought that we had found the back of Lisbon's Christmas tree—that mangy area turned to the wall, decorated with broken and unsightly ornaments that nevertheless had sentimental value—I spotted what I would come to love as one of Lisbon's most precious decorations: the sixteenth-century Church of Nossa Senhora da Saúde [Our Lady of Health]. What was it doing there? Rumor has it that in the midst of Salazar's obsession with hygiene and progress—the push to eradicate the Baixa Mouraria—the dictator spared the humble Baroque church, as he was pulled by the contrary political discourse of tradition.[4]

The ideological tug of war between the Estado Novo's modernization of Lisbon and glorification of Portugal's past is palpable in the Baixa Mouraria. Tradition, as anything but an abstract notion, has lost! Street names tell the stories of inhabitants long gone: the palm tree on Rua da Palma; the plumbing on Rua dos Canos; the butchery on Rua do Açougue (even the word *açougue* [butchery] has been replaced, in Portugal, by *talho* [butchery]); the mosque of the Islamic Chaplain on Rua do Capelão; the almond tree of Rua da Amendoeira; and the Well of the Fig Tree at Rua do Poço do Borratém. The Mouraria is rich in history and tradition archived in memory, however, in terms of architecture and urban planning, it is sad, decayed, abandoned, depressing.

"Where are the 'vibrant colors' and the 'whorish charms' of this Mouraria?" I asked myself that afternoon, as I was haunted by the innkeeper's warning.

On that trip, I saw a *fado vadio* performance—a more spontaneous Fado, without all of the folkloric trappings of the Bairro Alto's overpriced Fado houses—for the first time at the Mascote da Atalaia Bar. In 1993, I was too new to the Fado circuit to appreciate that I was listening to Fernando Maurício, "the King of Fado without a crown," who was singing about his Mouraria, where he had grown up:

Eu nasci na Mouraria
Na Rua do Capelão
Onde a Severa vivia
Onde o fado é tradição.[5]

[I was born in the Mouraria
On Rua do Capelão
Where [Maria] Severa lived
And where Fado is a tradition.]

When I returned to the United States, I was troubled by the incongruity of what I had seen in the Mouraria and the touching pride with which Maurício had sung of his neighborhood on that rainy January evening on Rua da Atalaia. On subsequent annual trips to Lisbon—and later biannual and entire summer trips—I made regular pilgrimages to the Mouraria to try to understand why a neighborhood that had almost been erased was so alive in the Portuguese collective conscience.

Regularly, I have returned to the somber Largo de Martim Moniz, and I have begun to understand that it is a work in progress, still in progress, barely a survivor of progress. I have spent hours in the Church of Nossa Senhora da Saúde: that Baroque gem that is testament to the humble grandeur of the lost Mouraria. I have wandered the *fadista* quarter, on Rua do Capelão, where Fernando Maurício grew up—across the street from the home where the Fado's most legendary singer, Maria Severa, had lived in the early nineteenth century—and near the street where the Fado's most recent star, Mariza, spent her childhood and adolescence. I have forced friends and family to accompany me to the Mouraria. Most of them thought that we had taken a wrong turn; they did not understand my fascination with the dark, tortuous alleys of the woeful quarter.

I have come to understand the *fadista* memory of the Mouraria, despite the architectural debauchery that threatens material tradition in Lisbon's riverside. This book is the product of years of trying to make sense of a recently demolished quarter that was one of the oldest of one of Europe's oldest capitals, yet, that persists in Lisbon's folkloric repertoire. Architectural historians speak briefly of the Estado Novo's demolition of the Mouraria within the context of the regime's greater plans for the expansion and modernization of Lisbon.[6] While their studies lament the sacrifice of a historical Lisbon, they view the amputation of the Mouraria as a necessary step in the capital's urban development.

I am not a critic of urban planning but rather of literary and cultural studies, therefore, for me, the poetic overshadows the pragmatic. When I see images of a traditional, pre-Republican Baixa Mouraria that was demolished for practical reasons in the name of progress, I realize that the historians have only told us one side of the story. The people's reactions, the outrage of the displaced inhabitants of the Mouraria, the sense of loss, and the regret of the city's lovers—in a word, the poetic—are echoed in the Fado. This book is about the Fado's strained voice: its protest, its mourning, and its grief regarding the murder of old Lisbon. It is in this voice that we find the construction and reconstruction of a lost Lisbon, and the writing and rewriting of a history that many did not want to hear.

Acknowledgments

PART OF MY SECOND CHAPTER WAS PUBLISHED BY THE CENTER FOR Portuguese Studies and Culture at the University of Massachusetts, Dartmouth as "Sousa do Casacão's 'Fado da Severa' and Júlio Dantas's *A Severa:* The Genesis of National Folklore in the Death of a Mouraria *Fadista*" (*Portuguese Literary and Cultural Studies* 16 [forthcoming]). A version of my fourth chapter was published by the Modern Humanities Research Association as "Gabriel de Oliveira's 'Há Festa na Mouraria' and the *Fado Novo*'s Criticism of the Estado Novo's Demolition of the Baixa Mouraria" (*Portuguese Studies* 20 [2004]: 134–51). Material from both chapters is reproduced with the written permission of the editors of the respective journals. All translations of Fados and Portuguese quotations are mine except where noted.

Apart from the portions of my second and fourth chapters that have appeared in print, I have only shared my work in draft with three people: my friend and mentor, Hortensia Morell of Temple University; my dear friend, Joanne Lucena of Arcadia University; and Victor Mendes of the University of Massachusetts, Dartmouth. I thank the three of them for their feedback and enthusiasm.

I would also like to express my gratitude to friends and places that, albeit indirectly, have nurtured me through this project.

I thank my mother, Marlyn Colvin, who taught me how to narrate, and my father, Ronald Colvin, who taught me how to reason.

I am grateful to my friends who have hosted me, and in whose homes parts of this book were written. Barry Pike and Paul Carey in Boston, Plymouth, and Provincetown—I love you guys; Ico Marques, Sylvie Zink, and Rui Zink in Lisbon; Christophe Vilaginès in Paris and Lisbon; and Stephanie Baum in London.

Thank you, Susana Catarina Borralho Correia, for your black-and-white photographs that capture the Mouraria's loss alongside its former beauty; and Vito Grillo, for having photographed and captured me in what, one day, will be my former beauty.

I thank Rui Afonso Santos for his autographed copy of Suzanne

Chantal's book, and for his invectives against Estado Novo architecture and Fado that have helped me develop an aesthetic apology for both. Ana and Steve Dyson welcomed me to their monthly potluck *tertúlias* whenever I was in Lisbon, and introduced me to a lively group of thinkers, willing to discuss anything over a meal. The Luso-American actress-turned-*fadista*, Michelle Pereira, called me to discuss "Fado Malhoa" and Maria Severa's biography after she had read my article in *Portuguese Literary and Cultural Studies*. Nathalie Drouglazet, a true colleague and friend, spent ten days with me in Lisbon, during which we shared Fados, Ginjinha, and war stories. *Obrigadinho*, Joãozinho Ferro and Harry's Bar where, despite the redecorating, hustlers still end up in fights with punters, Whores' Soup is *du jour*, and Amália's ghost hangs out with a knife in her garter belt . . . just in case. Thank you, Sylvie Zink, for having taught me to paint tiles. And, Christophe Vilaginès with whom I have sung Fados and discussed anecdotes about *fadistas*, and who gave me his copy of *Les amants du Tage*.

I would also like to thank a few friends who have engaged me with humor and encouragement when I have spoken about my research: Llorenç Comajoan, Isabel Estrada, Ginneh Flamer, Don Mumford, Meg Rider, Nancy Wong, and Jackie Zahn.

I would like to acknowledge some places in Lisbon that were and are truly *fadista*. I do not mean the Bairro Alto Fado houses where the singers roll their eyes as they lead a group a tourists into a tepid chorus of "Nem às Paredes Confesso"; rather, those places where the spirit of the *faia* is alive even when the Fado is not present. Some of these places have closed, but my brushes with them over the last fifteen years have helped me write this book about *fadista* Lisbon: Isaura and Jorge's Saturday-evening Fado association on Travessa do Oleiro; A Mascote da Atalia; A Tasca do Chico; Portas Largas; Finalmente; Memories das Tias; Rua do Arco do Carvalho; the nightly parade of transgendered prostitutes on Rua do Conde do Redondo; Mestre André when Jorge Pinho was alive; The Church of Nossa Senhora da Saúde; and the Casa-Museu do Fado e da Guitarra Portuguesa.

Oh, and *Guitarras de Lisboa . . . obrigado!*

The Reconstruction of Lisbon

Introduction: Progress, Tradition, Demolitions, and Overdue Outrage

As long as Pacheco is here, and as long as there's a house standing, the demolition will go on.

—Popular Saying

THE ESTADO NOVO'S PLANS FOR URBAN REHABILITATION IN LISBON, carried out by Duarte Pacheco's "Plano de Urbanização e Expansão da Cidade" and "Plano de Remodelação da Baixa," and Faria da Costa's "Salvação Barreto" program, justified the demolition of historic neighborhoods "condemned to progress," including the capital's oldest districts, Mouraria and Alfama.[1] However, just before Salazar's death in 1970, and the consequent shift in political regime as Portugal advanced to its April 25th Revolution, the "Salvação Barreto" program had lost its momentum. In 1940, national attention focused on the restoration of the Sé [Lisbon's Cathedral] and the Torre de Belém in preparation for the Exposição do Mundo Português [Portuguese-World Expo]. However, the Câmara Municipal de Lisboa [CML, Lisbon's city hall], did not propose a plan to protect the capital's architectural heritage until 1967. By then, the Baixa Mouraria had suffered the blows of the Estado Novo's progress. Plans to widen Rua da Palma and Avenida do Almirante Reis—first presented in 1852—were realized in the 1930s.[2] Between the 1930s and the 1960s, the Baixa Mouraria was demolished: the Palace of the Marquis of Alegrete in 1946; the Apolo Theatre in 1949; the Church of Socorro and the buildings to the west of Rua da Mouraria in 1956. In 1961, Lisboners reacted to the CML's neglect of the capital's architectural heritage when the Mouraria's only extant gates on the fourteenth-century Fernandine Wall—Portas de São Vicente da Mouraria/Arco do Marquês de Alegrete—were demolished.

Salazar's fall from his chair in 1968 facilitated explicit criticism of the Estado Novo's ideals, including a reevaluation of the regime's solutions for urban planning. But already in 1967, the CML had realized its error in demolishing the Baixa Mouraria. Lisbon's mayor, França Borges, and his 1967 "Plano Director de Lisboa," which proposed to define areas of historic preservation in the capital, was approved in 1970.[3] The Empresa Pública de Urbanização de Lisboa (EPUL) was founded in 1971 and the Serviço de Apoio Ambulatório Local (SAAL) in 1974.[4] The "Plano Director" of 1967, however, turned its back on the problem of Martim Moniz's void when in 1972, the CML abandoned the plans of Faria da Costa, Eduardo Paiva Lopes, and A. Barros de Fonseca to erect a plaza in the Baixa Mouraria. In 1974, the CML shifted the "Plano de Renovação Urbana de Martim Moniz" to the EPUL's hands. Between the 1970s and 1990s the EPUL worked with engineer, Ferro Gomes, and architects, Francisco Silva, Carlos Duarte, and José Lamas to replace the empty lots left by the "Salvação Barreto" program with the Centro Comercial Martim Moniz, mirrored by the Centro Comercial Mouraria, behind the sixteenth-century Church of Nossa Senhora da Saúde. And by the inauguration of the 1998 Expo, the CML had installed Moorish-inspired fountains in Largo de Martim Moniz.

The return to an Islamic motif seems appropriate in a neighborhood where toponyms signal mere ghosts of a past. Norberto de Araújo says of the Mouraria, "the Moors avenged themselves by leaving behind their name."[5] In a similar tradition, the Mouraria's parish still is known as Socorro, despite the demolition of the homonymous church in 1956. We enter the Mouraria from Praça da Figueira at the Rua do Arco do Marquês de Alegrete, although the arch was dismantled in 1961. And, still today, Lisboners refer to the criminally problematic Baixa Mouraria, surrounding the Martim Moniz metro station, as *o buraco*, although the hole left by the "Salvação Barreto" demolitions has been filled.

These nostalgic names signal the errors of the Estado Novo's progress while drawing our attention to the Baixa Mouraria's singular condition of existing only in memory, or rather, in a reconstructed memory. To the west of the Church of Nossa Senhora da Saúde, all architectural evidence of the former Baixa Mouraria has been leveled, save the crumbling vestiges of a tower from the 1373 Fernandine Wall on Rua da Palma. Yet, we do not deny that the Mouraria's role in Lisbon's history has been significant. It was the suburban commune of the Mozarabs in Moorish Lixbuna. Their homes, that served as the walled city's northern bulwark, were set on fire by the Anglo-Norman

The Mouraria and Largo de Martim Moniz as seen from the Outeiro da Graça, photograph by Susana Correia.

pilgrims during the 1147 Lisbon Siege. The site was the concession to the free Moors who swore fealty to Afonso Henriques in 1179.[6] After Dom Manuel I's expulsion of the Moors, the sixteenth-century Christian suburb fought the Plague by invoking St. Sebastian and Our Lady of Health in religious procession.[7] Camões had died in penury in the Mouraria, months before Portugal fell into Castille's hands. The Mouraria was incorporated as Lisbon's eighth quarter in the seventeenth century.[8] Simultaneously, it was home to nobility and a stage for prostitution and violent crime in the nineteenth century. And, finally, in the twentieth century, it was the ash and dust of a failed rehabilitation project: a lesson, for posterity, in how not to resolve urban problems in a historic quarter.[9]

Notwithstanding the district's many avatars during a residence of nearly twelve centuries, today the Mouraria connotes a picturesque distortion of its nineteenth-century reality. We associate the Mouraria with the splendor of its legends of bullfighting noblemen who courted singing prostitutes, despite that by the 1930s, the alluded Mouraria had disappeared. As early as 1938, Araújo remarks on his contemporaries' anachronistic vision of the Mouraria: "Long gone is the sordid character of the 'low life' that spread out up to the great artery of Rua da Mouraria, on to which the ignominious '*Rua Suja*' of last century belted out lowly Fados."[10] He adds, "today's Mouraria . . . associated with Portuguese guitars, knife wounds, whores, pianos in the parlor—no longer exists."[11] That Mouraria *does* exist in a commonly accepted folklore that aimed to rescue the quarter as the Estado Novo bulldozed it. As a result, the contemptible *fadista* Mouraria of knife-wielding ruffians and Rua do Capelão's brothels has been recontextualized as Lisbon folklore and is part of the Portuguese collective conscience.

My study concerns the genesis and proliferation of an artificial folkloric identity in a disappearing neighborhood in Lisbon. How and why did a degraded neighborhood, so seemingly devoid of folkloric charm that it was demolished, become the setting of some of Lisbon's fondest memories? Could the CML's leveling of the Mouraria between the 1930s and 1960s have created the need for a collective memory of the absent neighborhood?[12] What are the historical and cultural circumstances that have made the Mouraria a relevant neighborhood in Portuguese folklore?

Tourists in the Bairro Alto eat at the expensive restaurant, A Severa, named for the nineteenth-century Mouraria's most famous resident: a tubercular prostitute. Although several Fados of the mid-twentieth century narrate enchanted vignettes in the life of the Mouraria's Rosa Maria, Lisboners do not know that the character may have been inspired by a prostitute who lured punters into her bedroom so that her sailor boyfriend could ambush and rob them by jumping out of a closet with a knife. The setting of Portugal's first talkie, *A Severa* (1931), Rua do Capelão was known in the nineteenth century as *Rua Suja*. And while the Mouraria's "Dirty Street" may have overflowed with rosemary, it was indeed one of Lisbon's most dangerous corners, described at the turn of the twentieth century as "the thieves' hideout, where knife sharpeners entered with their donkeys, [yet] many of them disappeared without ever being heard from again"; or the street that "fights and sings; scratches, stabs and brandishes the fool's guitar," where "fighters and singers are at home."[13]

I trace the origins of the reconstruction of the nineteenth-century Mouraria to twentieth-century Portuguese popular culture and, in particular, to the *fado novo*'s need to assert its autonomy from fascistic aesthetics. The Fado's detractors have accused the national song of fostering Salazarian ideals and thus perpetuating the regime's oppressive notion of patriotism, as expressed by António Ferro, director of the Secretariado de Propaganda Nacional [SPN, Secretariat of National Propaganda] (1933–45): "Art, literature and the sciences constitute the great showpiece of national identity, it is what the outsider sees when looking in."[14] But the *fado novo* never fully divorced itself from its antisocial character of the nineteenth century and continued to lampoon society's absurdities in the twentieth. The lyricists, however, had to resort to allegory and metaphor to criticize the Estado Novo.

I understand the relationship between the *fado novo* and the aesthetics of the Estado Novo and Portuguese Fascism to be problematical; the Fado benefited from a privileged position during Salazar's regime, when it was subservient to the Estado Novo's concept of nationalism. In the early years of the Estado Novo, the SPN did not take a stance on the Fado. However, when the young journalist, António Ferro, interviewed Salazar in 1933, he revealed the key to the relationship between nationalism and art that would guide his direction of the SPN for the next twelve years: "If it is just and necessary to think about the preservation of our artistic heritage, it is equally just, and perhaps more urgent, to think about the living arts that should accompany our evolution, that should be the expression of our era."[15] Should the Fado be embraced by the regime and be considered the soundtrack to the evolution of the Estado Novo, it would have to suppress its subversive character, mold itself to the aesthetics of Salazarian art, and consent to being a vehicle for fascistic propaganda.

Vieira Nery remarks that "the regime, at its highpoint, tolerates Fado performances . . . when they are controlled with respect to their venues and routines, and to their poetic and ideological content."[16] However, in 1952, Salazar tells his biographer that he does not like the Fado because it is depressing and "has a softening influence on the Portuguese character" and it "sap[s] all energy from the soul and lead[s] to inertia."[17] Thus the Estado Novo allowed the Fado to thrive in massive popular contexts, such as comedy films of the 1930s and 1940s, in which the song promoted the regime's image of *bairrismo* [neighborhood traditions], and its characterization of Lisbon's *pobretes mas alegretes* [poor but happy] inhabitants. Performative and plastic art under the Estado Novo washed over the social problems of Lisbon's impoverished riverside by distracting its residents with the contradictory lure of myths of tradition alongside the promise of progress.

Vieira Nery identifies the Fado's return to the nineteenth-century

Mouraria as complicity with the Estado Novo's repressive nostalgia: "Now the Fado evokes Severa, Cesária, Júlia Florista, Rosa Maria and all of the great mythic figures of its pioneer era."[18] Indeed the regime encouraged *saudosismo* [nostalgia] as a strategy to divert the working class's attention from economic difficulties, and thus served to censor subversive lyrics that might criticize the Estado Novo. Nevertheless, this *saudade* implies a rejection of the present in its idealization of the past. Vieira Nery comments, "the Fado insists on declaring itself as a sort of last chance for an idealized historic tradition, opposed, by definition, to modernity and to contemporary political intervention."[19]

I propose that the *fado novo*, and other popular cultural expressions related to the Fado—Portuguese cinema, musical theatre and political cartoons—have undermined the will of the Estado Novo by denouncing the modernization of Lisbon, and thus questioning the regime's notion of progress by way of the glorification of a pre-Republican Mouraria: the very Mouraria that the twentieth-century urban rehabilitation projects hoped to demolish. The Fado seized the opportunity in the imminent void caused by the demolition of the Mouraria, or rather the erasing of its material history, to rewrite its own saga in its rewriting of the history of Lisbon. My study addresses Portuguese popular culture's reaction to the coetaneous trends in urban development that have ignored the historical significance of Lisbon's riverside. I shall examine the *fado novo*'s successful recontextualization of the sordid pre-Republican Mouraria—characterized by prostitution, knife-fights, and petty crime—as sanitized Portuguese folklore. I conclude that the covertly subversive lyrics of the *fado novo* of 1931 to 1974 are responsible for having reconstructed the nineteenth-century Mouraria that continues to be accepted as part of Lisbon's historical-folkloric identity.

But the Fado does not bear all blame for the picturesque restoration of the decadent Mouraria. The effectiveness of the *fado novo*'s critical lyrical tropes implies the audience's complicity. The success of the Fado's subversive criticism of the Estado Novo depends on the song's mirroring the opinions of the public; the Fado's outrage vis-à-vis the demolition of the Baixa Mouraria reflects the outrage felt by Lisboners. Furthermore, the motif of the romanticized pre-Republican Mouraria exceeded urban boundaries and appealed to a national audience for whom Lisbon's Mouraria otherwise might not mean anything. I attribute the proliferation of the Fado's motif of the pre-

Republican Mouraria to a national longing for the past as a means to criticize the Estado Novo. Because the theme of *saudade* is central to the *fado novo,* its manifestation within the context of a disappearing Mouraria seems inoffensive. Twentieth-century lyricists recognized the leitmotif of *saudade* in recent Fados and benefited from the emotion's capacity to denounce the present in light of a glorious past.[20] The *fado novo,* therefore appeared to adhere to a Portuguese aesthetics: the longing of the *cantigas d'amigo* or Camões's spleen in exile. Nevertheless, the recontextualized *saudade* questioned the judgment of the State by accusing the "Salvação Barreto" program of ignoring the past. The Fado points its finger at the regime's paradoxes, signaling the cannibalization of its ideals: progress implies the sacrifice of a heroic national history. Yet, because public resentment about a local cause provided a relatively safe forum in which to criticize the regime, the subversive intentions of the lyrics that alluded to the nineteenth-century Mouraria were not perceived as such, even when expressed in the national song and thus embraced by the entire nation.

Political cartoons of the late 1940s to early 1960s indicate popular opposition to the "Salvação Barreto" project as not just a Lisboner's concern, but as a Portuguese concern. Most cartoons exploit the fascistic obsession with Portuguese history by suggesting that the demolition of the Mouraria threatens the nation's heroic past. Other satirists signal intrinsic irony in the Estado Novo's plans for progress: the demolition of the cradle of the Fado. The regime's plans for urban renewal jeopardize Salazar's patriotic trinity of the "F"s (Fado, *futebol,* and Fátima) by bulldozing Lisbon's most *fadista* quarter. Others criticize the demolition projects through the lyrics of easily recognizable Fados. By appropriating the musical form consecrated by the Estado Novo, the humorists turn the tables on the political regime.

The humor of the political cartoons is a pretext for the common thread that links it to other forms of popular culture: an evocation of a *fadista* Mouraria that had disappeared before the demolition projects of the 1930s. While the cartoonists' apparent criticism focuses on the misguided "Salvação Barreto" program, indeed their images recall a Mouraria that was not destroyed by the Estado Novo's urban rehabilitation.

Why blame the Estado Novo, even if in masked language, for modernization that already had begun to take place before 1910?

The Fado was a relatively young musical genre, dating only as far back as D. João VI's return to the Continent from Rio de Janeiro. The song's association with marginalized sectors in society provoked more scornful criticism than praise. Most pre-Republican and first-Republican intellectuals—including Eça de Queiroz and Teófilo Braga—treated the problem of the Fado in Lisbon as an unfortunate condition of Portuguese urban society. The Fado's contextualization among the Mouraria's popular/criminal element hindered the song's acceptance outside of its own milieu, with the exception, of course, of the passing fad of the daring nobility who slummed in the Mouraria and brought the local *fadistas* to sing with piano in salons, at the bullring or at the bucolic suburban picnics, the so-called *frescatas fora de portas.*

Cascais *fadista,* Rodrigo comments on the nineteenth-century nobility's forays into Lisbon's popular quarters and their impact on the reputation of the Fado:

> [At the end of the nineteenth century], there were . . . many noblemen who had their clandestine lovers and so they went out at night, listened to Fado, mingled with the masses—because it was mostly among the masses that they went to look for their lovers—and so, sometimes they were caught with whores who put on airs of being great *fadistas,* but they were not, obviously not at all. It took many years for the Fado to overcome that reputation because it bred the notion that only indigents, vagrants, prostitutes, the wayward were the ones who sang the Fado, which, in part, is true, but you really cannot generalize.[21]

In effect, the demolition of the Mouraria was the demolition of the material evidence of the Fado's sordid past. The erasing of this past afforded *fadistas* the opportunity to elevate the song's reputation in the urban, and later, the national psyche, and Lisbon had little testimony to contradict such a history of the Fado. Given the opportunity, the Fado repainted its self-portrait in the pinks and blues of Roque Gameiro's watercolors, populated with Bordalo Pinheiro's benevolent drunkards and Malhoa's repentant prostitutes.

And let's not forget Júlio Dantas's Rua do Capelão!

The recontextualization of the decadent pre-Republican Mouraria as urban folklore takes shape at the turn of the twentieth century in eyewitness and second-hand histories that expose Lisbon's underbelly while observing Rua do Capelão's prostitutes with compassion. José Pinto de Carvalho's *História do Fado* (1903) and Alberto Pimentel's *A Triste Canção do Sul* (1904) boast of Maria Severa and her contemporaries as *provocateuses* of outdated duels in their reconstruction of a

Mouraria of the previous generation. These histories, which consist of interviews with Severa, remembered conversations with the ruffians of Rua do Capelão and Rua da Amendoeira, and memories of the *fadista* Mouraria, vindicate the Fado's image in Lisbon's collective conscience and propose serious historical inquiry of the milieu of the Mouraria's bordellos.[22]

Since Teófilo Braga catalogued Sousa do Casacão's eulogy to Maria Severa, "O Fado da Severa" (1848), in the *Cancioneiro Popular* (1867), the prostitute's legend has clouded the Fado's interpretation of its own history.[23] Pinto de Carvalho refers to Severa as "inspiration for one of the oldest Fados, but whose biography has been twisted out of shape."[24] Pimentel adds, "if everybody is still talking about Severa, it is, without doubt, that today's generation has only a vague, fleeting notion, fed only by Fado songs."[25] But the *fado novo* of the mid-twentieth century does not merely continue a tradition begun by Sousa do Casacão's verses; rather, it elaborates on an isolated nineteenth- and early twentieth-century literary fascination with the figure of the Mouraria *fadista.* Before Júlio Dantas created Severa's popular incarnation in his novel, *A Severa* (1901), and drama, *A Severa: Peça em Quatro Actos* (1901), the *fadista* had been mentioned in Camilo Castelo Branco's *Noites de Insónia* (1874) and *Eusébio Macário* (1879).[26] Luís Augusto Palmeirim's interview with Severa at her apartment in the Bairro Alto, in *Os Excêntricos do Meu Tempo* (1891) had traced sketches of the *fadista* that would serve as the foundations for her specious biographies.[27] And Eça de Queiroz's ambivalence toward the Mouraria *fadistas* of the nineteenth century had surfaced in his essays and fiction.[28]

Dantas's *A Severa,* however, has altered twentieth-century Portuguese popular culture's image of the nineteenth-century Mouraria *fadista* by identifying Maria Severa as an emblem of both the Mouraria and Portugal, thus cultivating a sympathetic relationship between the nation and the degraded quarter of Lisbon. Three decades later, when the author collaborates on the soundtrack for José Leitão de Barros's cinematic adaptation of *A Severa* (1931), he reiterates Maria Severa and the Mouraria Fado as emblems of Portugal and thus grants license to later Fado lyricists to elevate the urban song in the national psyche, at the very moment when the CML breaks ground to initiate its demolition of the Baixa Mouraria.

Fado lyricists seize on Dantas's forging of Severa as a national heroine and the Fado as the national song to manifest a sub-rosa criticism of the Estado Novo's demolition of the Mouraria between the 1930s and 1970s. The lyricists exploit Dantas's fictionalization of Severa's life, death, and consequent legacy in its attempt to link Severa's Mouraria and the Fado to the Portuguese character, to evoke national sympathy or even outrage for the local cause of the erasing of the Mouraria. In the *fado novo*'s recontextualization of Dantas's Mouraria, we observe a criticism of the imminent destruction of the Mouraria's three faces: the *fadista*, the aristocratic, and the Christian. The lyrics of the *fado novo* of the 1930s to 1970s lament the demolitions that have taken place and warn against further erasing Dantas's Mouraria.

In chapter 1, I outline the genesis of Dantas's play and novel to understand the relationship between his literary avatars and their real-life counterparts. I consider portraits of Severa that had been traced prior to the 1901 debut of Dantas's play—that might have served as inspiration for his character—and criticism of the author's Romantic sketch of the nineteenth-century Mouraria. I argue that because of the diffusion of Dantas's *A Severa*, in musical theater (1909) and cinematic adaptations (1931), and because the inception of Portuguese radio in the 1930s coincided with the success of Dantas's "Novo Fado da Severa (Rua do Capelão)" (1931), Dantas's Severa has become Portugal's Severa, and, consequently, Dantas's Mouraria is Portugal's Mouraria.

Chapter 2 considers the genesis of the nineteenth-century Mouraria *fadista* as a national icon in twentieth-century Portuguese popular culture. In his drama, Dantas establishes a metaphoric correlation between Maria Severa, the Mouraria, the Fado, and Portugal, when his heroine dies in the arms of the Fado, thus realizing the fate of all Portuguese (according to Dantas's protagonist, the Count of Marialva). Dantas's mise en scène of Severa's death is followed by the refrain from Sousa do Casacão's "Fado da Severa": the last lines of the play. *Fado novo* lyricists of the 1930s to 1970s recontextualize Sousa do Casacão's lyrics and Dantas's proposal of a folkloric Mouraria—the cradle of the national song—to elevate the urban song in the Portuguese collective conscience. The *fado novo* proposes that Severa's death is the death of the Fado, the Mouraria, and Portugal. In such a scheme, the Estado Novo has the opportunity to preserve for posterity the cradle of the defunct Fado by salvaging the remains of the Mouraria's architectural patrimony. Therefore, the Estado Novo's demolition of the Mouraria is observed as an unpatriotic gesture that deprives the Portuguese of their fate to die in the arms of their national song.

In chapter 3, I examine the cultural legacy of Dantas's fictionalization of Severa's romance with the Count of Vimioso to conclude that our folkloric notion of the nineteenth-century Mouraria is based on Dantas's novelistic and theatrical treatment of history. I argue that *fado novo* lyricists appropriate Dantas's love affair between the nobleman and the prostitute to recall a Mouraria that is in danger of extinction: the seemingly egalitarian nineteenth-century Mouraria, characterized by class mingling between aristocracy and *fadistas.* The *fado novo* insists on Dantas's memory of a Mouraria in which class stratification crumbled, as a means to signal the irony of the Estado Novo's goals for progress: the demolition of the architecture of a socially unstratified Mouraria to make way for modern housing projects that will unite the poor and the bourgeoisie in the same neighborhood.

And finally, in chapter 4, I study the legacy of Severa as an archetype of the prostitute from Rua do Capelão. I argue that the *fado novo* exploits Dantas's characterization of a virtuous prostitute, who lives and dies in a morally ambivalent Mouraria, as a last resort to recall Lisbon's attention to the pious, Christian Mouraria so often forgotten when we evoke a *fadista* or aristocratic Mouraria. Gabriel de Oliveira's quasi-historical figure of the prostitute, Rosa Maria, in the Fado "Há Festa na Mouraria," constitutes a reincarnation of Dantas's Severa. Rosa Maria functions as a double for Severa, and by reappearing in several Fados posterior to Oliveira's, she becomes yet another manifestation of the Mouraria's complex nature: at once sordid and holy. The appropriation of Oliveira's character of Rosa Maria—who is associated with the Procession of the Church of Nossa Senhora da Saúde, a permanent reminder of the pre-Republican architecture that has been sacrificed in the name of the Estado Novo's progress—serves to criticize the "Salvação Barreto" rehabilitation program as it aims to save the endangered Mouraria from further demolitions of the *fadista* quarter.

My book asks why the Mouraria is still such a relevant and iconic neighborhood in Portugal's folkloric memory, despite the quarter's near obliteration in the twentieth-century "Salvação Barreto" urban rehabilitation program. We find the answer to this question in Portuguese popular culture of the 1930s to 1970s. In the lyrics of the twentieth-century *fado novo,* we witness the folkloric reconstruction of a *fadista,* noble, and Christian Mouraria, all rooted in Júlio Dantas's construction of Severa's early nineteenth-century Lisbon.

1

Júlio Dantas's *A Severa:* The Genesis of the Folkloric Figure of the Mouraria Prostitute

> Portuguese melancholy is a sort of national flower, cultivated and watered by sentimental literature and a misunderstood lyricism of traditions, of which the Fado is its most noxious expression.
>
> —Dr. Augusto de Castro

DANTAS'S CHARACTERIZATION OF MARIA SEVERA HAS CONFOUNDED critics' understanding of the *fadista*'s biography throughout the twentieth century. Pinto de Carvalho remarks, "we have too much faith in the crude legend that grew out of the name of that streetwalker, a legend embellished by popular fantasies and the connivance of novelists."[1] Pimentel notes that "through the muddled mist of oral history," Dantas traces sketches of Severa and the Count of Vimioso "faded by the passage of time."[2] And as late as 1994, Sucena comments, "we are indebted to Júlio Dantas for the legend, romanticized as it may be, of that unique feminine figure, whose name has been linked forever to the Fado."[3]

Pimentel and Pinto de Carvalho gloss what they consider Dantas's artistic distortions by referring their readers to Severa's contemporaries, Palmeirim and Queriol. Pinto de Carvalho vows to "set the record straight about the life of the mezzo-soprano of the conservatories of vice."[4] In a similar tone, Pimentel declares, "the legend is good; but history is better."[5] Sucena confirms that even within *fadista* circles, many believed that Severa was a figment of Dantas's imagination.[6] And the Fado "Maria Severa" asks us of the late *fadista:* "Sabem quem era? / Talvez ninguém" [Does anyone know who she was? / Perhaps nobody].[7] But is the demand to discredit Dantas's picturesque Severa warranted? To what extent is Dantas's Maria Severa a fictional creation? In 1938, Norberto de Araújo argues that whether Dantas exaggerated the *fadista*'s celebrity, certainly Severa "was 'someone' in her day, the days of the turbulent, *fadista*, picturesque Bairros Altos and Mourarias," but that Lisbon's popular quarters of the mid-nineteenth century "were more suited to acid-based etchings than to naïve watercolors."[8]

What do we know about Maria Severa Onofriana? She was born on July 26, 1820 to Severo Manuel de Sousa and Ana Gertrudes Severa in Anjos.[9] She lived with her mother, Barbuda, above her tavern on Rua da Madragoa (Rua de Vicente Borga). In 1844 or 1845, Severa had lived in a small apartment on Travessa do Poço da Cidade in the Bairro Alto, before she and Barbuda moved to Rua da Amendoeira in the Mouraria, to a house that belonged to Severa's lover, the thirteenth Count of Vimioso, D. Francisco de Paula de Portugal e Castro. Severa spent her last days in a house on the corner of Rua do Capelão and Beco do Forno. And she died of a stroke, at age twenty-six, on November 30, 1846.[10]

And then there are the legendary anecdotes about Severa. We suppose that her mother, a Spanish gypsy who had come to Portugal in a caravan, began to prostitute Severa when she was twelve years old.[11] While she lived in the Bairro Alto, Severa sang in the Mouraria at the Rosária dos Óculos tavern, on Rua do Capelão, where a soldier, O Chico do 10, fell in love with her. When Chico learned that Severa had deceived him with another punter, he stabbed his rival to death and washed his knife off in the Socorro fountain. Upon hearing of Severa's association with the crime, the Count of Vimioso—who had been Barbuda's lover—courted the prostitute at the Rosária dos Óculos tavern. Perhaps motivated by jealousy or by a sense of decorum, the Count kept Severa on the second floor of a house on Rua do Benformoso, from which she escaped by jumping into a passing laundry wagon. The *fadista* was found singing in either the Bairro Alto or the Mouraria. In 1846, the twenty-six-year-old *fadista* died while choking on a meal of pigeon and wine. When the Count of Vimioso learned of the death of his recently estranged Severa, he was devastated:

> O Conde de Vimioso
> Ai! Quase que enlouqueceu
> Quando lhe foram dizer
> A Severa já morreu.[12]

[The Count of Vimioso
Oh! He nearly went mad
When they told him
That Severa was dead.]

Despite Pinto de Carvalho's *amende honorable* and Pimentel's proposal to put aside the *fadista*'s legend, these authors ignore that some of Dantas's theatrical and novelistic embellishments of a few years earlier coincide with the biographies of Severa in *História do Fado* and *A Triste Canção do Sul.*[13] Dantas's recounting of Severa's life can be traced to the same sources that Pimentel and Pinto de Carvalho deem as the dependable foundation of their histories; Dantas's characterization of the *fadista* synthesizes the inconclusiveness of the oral tradition and Palmeirim's and Queriol's biographical accounts.[14] Dantas's ambivalent portrait of Severa—at times a silver-tongued virago, at times timid and gracious—constitutes a composite sketch of the conflicting reports of Severa's interviewers.[15] In their criticism of Severa's literary avatars, Pinto de Carvalho and Pimentel overlook Dantas's piecing together fragments of Severa's contemporaries' testimony to present an objective vision, however idealized, of the singer. Dantas did not exaggerate Severa's portrait; rather, he filled in the gaps of the scant biographical data on the streetwalker to create the folkloric figure of the Mouraria *fadista* / prostitute. Thirty years later, Leitão de Barros would comment, "one thing is the myth, 'the colorful poetic figure' of Severa, and another is the reality of those 'three lines' of her biography"; nevertheless, "the confrontation between myth and reality always teaches us something useful."[16] Júlio de Sousa e Costa speculates that if Severa had lived as late as the 1930s, her biography would have appeared in Portugal's most popular newspapers.[17] However, because she did not live so late, our early twenty-first-century understanding of Severa's biography depends on, and is indebted to, Dantas's intersection between myth and history.

Dantas gives us two versions of Severa's life. The dramatic, *A Severa: Peça em Quatro Actos*, focuses on the vicissitudes of the *fadista*'s relationship with the Count (of Marialva) in 1846, the year of Severa's death. The novel, *A Severa*'s first chapter, begins in the Mouraria, when Maria Severa is eight years old. Through flashback, we learn of Barbuda's flight from Spain and arrival in the Mouraria. The novel narrates Severa's fatalistic entry into a life of prostitution in the Bairro Alto and the Mouraria, where she meets the Count and abandons him for the Fado. The novel and the play end with Severa's death and the Mouraria's mourning its loss.

Later characterizations of the nineteenth-century *fadista* remit us to Dantas's dramatic and novelistic Severas. Already by 1910, we observe the impact of André Brun's contemporary operetta adaptation of Dantas's *A Severa* (1909) on José Malhoa's painting *O Fado* (1910).[18] The coincidence between Malhoa's and Dantas's representations of the *fadista* / prostitute has provoked misinterpretations of the artist's subjects, Adelaide da Facada and Amâncio, as Severa and Sousa do Casacão.[19] The *fado mouraria*, "Cinco Quinas" alludes that Severa's Mouraria is the background for the painting:

Mouraria mãe do fado
Que Malhoa quis pintar
Triste canção que nasceu
Para sofrer a cantar.[20]

[Mouraria mother of the Fado
That Malhoa tried to paint
A sad song that was born
To suffer while singing.]

"Fado Malhoa" identifies Severa as the feminine figure in *O Fado:*

Dali vos digo que eu ouvi
A voz que se esmera
Boçal dum faia banal
Cantando à Severa.[21]

[I tell you that, in that painting,
I heard the perfect voice
Of a simple, common *fadista*
Who was singing to Severa.]

Adelaide da Facada has been confused with Severa in twentieth-century cartoons that parody Malhoa's painting. In Pinto de Magalhães's cartoon, "Um Desastre. 'A Severa' . . . Já Morreu" [Disaster. "A Severa" . . . Is Dead], Maria Severa is wearing the same skirt that Adelaide da Facada wears in Malhoa's painting.[22] Francisco Valença's caricature "O Legado José Malhôa" [José Malhoa's Legacy], satirizes the painting *O Fado* through a parody of the lyrics of Sousa do Casacão's "Fado da Severa."[23] And Stuart Carvalhais's "No Centenário de Mestre Malhoa" [On the Centenary of Master Malhoa] reads: "Maria in a Severe situation has always had 'Zé Fadista' as a great accompanyist!"[24]

Even art historian, José-Augusto França, basing his observations on Sousa Pinto's study of *O Fado*, has mistaken Malhoa's femme fatale for Severa.[25] And Amália Rodrigues's role as Severa in the 1955 stage production of Dantas's play resembles her portrayal of Adelaide da Facada, as she sings "Fado Malhoa," from within the 1910 painting in Augusto Fraga's 1947 video clip.[26]

But the coincidence between Malhoa's rendering of Adelaide da Facada and Dantas's descriptions of Severa is not due solely to the creativity of the author. We observe similarities between Malhoa's prostitute and Palmeirim's Severa: "She was smoking, reclining on a straw chaise longue, wearing pointy, patent leather slippers."[27] And Palmeirim's details of Severa's bedroom are mimicked in Malhoa's painting: "Hanging from the wall (a common sacrilege in houses of that sort) a horrid etching representing the Passion of our Lord."[28] We might say that Dantas turned Palmeirim's anecdote into literary folklore and Malhoa tailored it to the plastic arts.

If *A Severa* determined for the twentieth century the folkloric image of the nineteenth-century Mouraria *fadista*, Dantas's theatrical and novelistic setting of Rua do Capelão served as a precedent for Portuguese popular culture's treatment of the Mouraria, characterized by "the regal sadness of that disgraced quarter."[29] The novelty of Leitão de Barros's filmic adaptation of *A Severa* (1931) thus would make Dantas's Mouraria Portugal's Mouraria. That is, Portugal saw the Mouraria for the first time through Dantas's eyes and Leitão de Barros's lens. Jorge Cid's cartoon, "1901–1932," signals the impact of Dantas's *A Severa: Peça em Quatro Actos* and Leitão de Barros's *A Severa* on two generations: "The carnival costumes of 1901 . . . suffered the influence of the play 'A Severa' that, at the time, was on stage. As the carnival season approaches, we can see that the festivities of 1932 are suffering the influence of the same drama, now on film."[30]

The cinematic *A Severa* coincided with the CML's wrecking ball's first incursion into the Mouraria. By the time of the city's projects to widen Rua da Palma and Avenida do Almirante Reis, the Portuguese recognized the lyrics of Dina Teresa's version of "Novo Fado da Severa (Rua do Capelão)" from the soundtrack of Leitão de Barros's film:

Ó, Rua do Capelão
Juncada de rosmaninho
Se o meu amor vier cedinho
Eu beijo as pedras do chão
Que ele pisar no caminho.[31]

[Oh, Rua do Capelão
Overflowing with rosemary
Should my lover arrive early
I shall kiss the pebbles
Of the ground on which he walks.]

Thus Rua do Capelão's true setting of knife fights and dangerous brothels mingled with the image of the street "overflowing with rosemary," so much that in 1943, Araújo described Rua do Capelão "walled in by rosemary."[32] And even today, two pots of rosemary decorate the entrance to Rua do Capelão—renamed Largo da Severa—on Rua da Mouraria: evidence of the perpetuation of Dantas's and Leitão de Barros's visions of the nineteenth-century Mouraria—a gesture relevant, today, perhaps only to those who recognize Dina Teresa's Fado.[33]

For a brief period, in the late 1920s and 1930s, the *fado novo* complied with the image of a modern Lisbon, and thus benefited from the CML's neglect of the Mouraria. We might say that the *fado novo* was the soundtrack for the Estado Novo's urban rehabilitation of Lisbon. Dina Teresa sang at the inauguration of the Retiro da Severa (1933) at the new Parque Eduardo VII.[34] And, as the CML prepared for the demolition of the Mouraria, Fado houses appeared in the Bairro Alto, Praça da Alegria and on Avenida da Liberdade.[35] The demolition of the Baixa Mouraria took the Fado out of its ghetto and made it available to all of Lisbon; thus began the sanitization of the national song and related urban folklore.

As *A Severa* was Portugal's first talkie, it made an aesthetic impact on Portuguese film during the 1930s through the 1950s. The Secretariado de Propaganda Nacional and the renamed Secretariado Nacional de Informação [SNI, National Secretariat of Information] profited from Leitão de Barros's and Dantas's images of the Mouraria of "*fadistas* and coachmen, of noblemen and 'severas,'" and promoted similar, yet ingenuine images of the quarter in Portuguese movies, despite that by 1943, all that remained of that Mouraria were "echoes of anecdotes, panoramic views, little paintings, etchings, watercolors with white backgrounds, a few somber brush strokes."[36]

The Fado accompanied mainstream Portuguese cinema of the 1930s through the 1950s. Portuguese film featured *fadistas* turned actors who often played *fadistas*. And as the decadent historic quarters of Lisbon's riverside were the obvious loci in movies such as *A Canção de Lisboa* (1933), *O Pátio das Cantigas* (1942), *O Costa do Castelo* (1943), *Fado, História d'uma Cantadeira* (1947), and *Rosa de Alfama* (1953), the directors reconstructed the popular neighborhoods in a picturesque form to distract the Portuguese from the reality that the Mouraria was being converted to rubble, and Alfama might be next!

Was the Fado the people's easy escape? Was its role in Portuguese film that of the people's only air hole in a constricted society?[37] Bénard da Costa warns against dismissing *nacional-cançonetismo* [Portuguese musical films] between 1939 and 1947 as propaganda by the regime to disguise national problems by exploiting the Fado as "opium for the masses."[38] That is, profit, combined with escapism, may have propelled *nacional-cançonetismo* films. Prior to the success of *Capas Negras* and *Fado, História d'uma Cantadeira* in 1947, of the four colossal money makers of Portuguese cinema—*A Severa*, *A Canção de Lisboa*, *As Pupilas do Senhor Reitor* and *Aldeia de Roupa Branca*—only *As Pupilas* did not contain elements of the *comédia revisteira* [musical review].[39] As Leitão de Barros's *A Severa* had been seen by over two hundred thousand people during its six months at the box office in 1931–32, its formula of combining the Lisbon Fado with recognizable images of Portuguese life would be imitated in Portuguese cinema through the mid-1960s.

As the Estado Novo took advantage of Dantas's and Leitão de Barros's Romantic portrayal of misery and presented it to the Portuguese as urban folklore, the *fado novo* followed. During the early stages of the CML's dismantling of the Baixa Mouraria, the SPN, Portuguese film, and the *fado novo* appeared to conspire to promote a vision of the nineteenth-century Mouraria alien to the reality of the quickly disappearing neighborhood. After all, the promised progress implicit in the demolition of the popular quarters would benefit the *fado novo* by allowing it to link its history to a respectable neighborhood with a colorful past.

But Lisboners soon realized that the scenes of progress promoted by the CML's propaganda films, such as *Melhoramentos Citadinos* (1931), were reserved for the more affluent neighborhoods to the west (Avenida da Liberdade, Restelo, and Belém) and the socially stratified housing projects to the north of the Mouraria (Alameda, Alvalade, and Areeiro) that reflected "the unhappy tastes of a social class defined by an economic power that sustained the regime."[40]

What went wrong?

In the 1940s, Faria da Costa was contracted to continue Duarte Pacheco's rehabilitation of Belém where the late Minister of Public Works had constructed a low-income housing project. Faria da Costa's plan, however, developed into free-standing homes for the rich. Today many of these homes host foreign embassies.[41] In a similar manner, Faria da Costa's Bairro de Alvalade (1945) proposed to solve the housing problem caused by the demolition of the Baixa Mouraria, during the widening of Rua da Palma into Avenida do Almirante Reis, by building homes that would integrate a variety of classes in the same neighborhood. França comments: "Among the luxurious tall buildings with high rents or the sad modesty of small houses asphyxiated in the alien city, these neighborhoods intended to reconcile tastes and interests, needs and burdens with varied success that would mark the zone as an autonomous city, independent from nineteenth-century Lisbon in many economic and social aspects, an image that would annex its inhabitants and consumers to a secondary position."[42] However, Maria Júlia Ferreira indicates, "the most valuable properties were located near the main roads and everything else in the more remote areas, which resulted in evident social stratification."[43] And as Duarte Pacheco's and Faria da Costa's demolitions chipped away at the cradle of the Fado, Dantas's Mouraria—Rua do Capelão, Largo da Guia and Rua da Amendoeira—was in danger of extinction.

The *fado novo* of the 1940s reflected the *fadistas*' sense of opportunity in the Mouraria's oblivion during the Estado Novo's rehabilitation projects. The demolition and the implicit displacement of the Mouraria's residents allowed the *fado novo* to recontextualize Dantas's and Leitão de Barros's Romantic Mouraria as a historical reality. The sordid pre-Republican Mouraria would recede, and the sanitized "nest of severas"—evoked by Dantas's words and Leitão de Barros's images—would characterize the Mouraria.[44] Already in 1938, Araújo demonstrates the association between the Mouraria and Dantas's Severa in his lamentation: "The Fado that [Maria Severa] knew how to sing with her heart in her throat—has come and gone. Let's not cry for her, let's evoke her spirit, after all we are in the Mouraria."[45]

By the 1946 leveling of the Palace of the Marquis of Alegrete, the *fado novo* had begun to betray its implied pact with Salazar's regime and the SNI, as the song assumed the guise of folklore to criticize the

Estado Novo's demolition of the Mouraria. Examples of critical discourse masked by innocuous lyrical tropes abound in the *fado novo* of the 1940s to 1960s. "Já Não Vou à Mouraria" is disguised as the narration of a spurned woman's evasion of her lover:

Já não vou à Mouraria
Pra não ver certa janela
Onde não estou dentro dela
Que triste verdade.[46]

[I no longer go to the Mouraria
To avoid seeing a certain window
I am not inside that window
It's sad but true.]

However, we may read between the lines her alienation from the transformed Mouraria:

Pode ser que eu algum dia
Volte lá mas muito tarde
Deixou de ser Mouraria
Pra mim é saudade.

[Maybe one day
I shall return, but not soon
The Mouraria no longer exists
For me it is just a nostalgic memory.]

"Ai, Mouraria" appears to be a love song imbued with nostalgia for Severa's Mouraria:

Ai, Mouraria
Das procissões a passar
Da Severa em voz saudosa
Na guitarra a soluçar.[47]

[Oh, Mouraria
With processions' passing by
With Severa in a nostalgic voice
In a sobbing Portuguese guitar.]

Yet the verses constitute a subversive nostalgic reference to a pre-Republican Mouraria as part of a campaign to denounce the "Salvação

Barreto" demolition projects by appealing to national historic sensibilities. Can we ignore that the Fado remarks on the CML's widening of Rua da Palma / Avenida do Almirante Reis?:

> Ai, Mouraria
> Da velha Rua da Palma
> Onde eu um dia
> Deixei presa a minh'alma.
>
> [Oh, Mouraria
> Of old Rua da Palma
> Where one day
> I left my soul captive.]

In its reference to Rua da Palma, the *fado novo* questions not only the government's transformation of one of Lisbon's oldest neighborhoods, but also the implicit erasing of Portugal's heroic past. The *fado novo* thus exploits the Estado Novo's preoccupation with Portugal's *Reconquista* by reminding the regime that it is tampering with the site of the Lisbon Siege's first miracle: Rua da Palma, where in 1147, a palm tree grew at the site of a fallen Anglo-Norman pilgrim. The sacrifice of Lisbon's tradition is the price of the Estado Novo's progress.

The *fado novo*'s lyricists, however, are aware of their privileged position in Salazar's regime and are careful to explore means of deceiving the censor in their criticism of the Estado Novo's dream of progress.[48] The composers subvert the regime's identification with the Fado as the national song by exploiting the Estado Novo's favor. The *fado novo* cultivates its own identity as the national song, thus undermining Salazar's conditional patronage of the Fado; the Fado is the national song whether the regime approves, and whether the Fado promotes the regime's image of *bairrismo*.

However, the *fado novo* is not reacting merely to the Estado Novo's propagandistic designs on the song; rather, the Fado's lyricists are perpetuating Dantas's own proposal to elevate the song in the national psyche. In his recontextualization of the nineteenth-century Mouraria in the Romantic memory of the early twentieth, Dantas forges a metaphoric relationship between the Mouraria, Severa, and the Fado. Because Dantas's vision of the nineteenth-century Mouraria is the country's first image of the quarter, presented as massive popular culture, *A Severa* guarantees automatic national identification between

Rua da Palma, photograph by Susana Correia.

the Mouraria and the *fadista*. Severa declares to the gypsy, Romão: "The Mouraria is neither here nor there. . . . It is wherever I am! Wherever I go, it tags along. I am the Mouraria!"[49] Dantas complicates his metaphor when Severa claims: "I am the Fado!"[50] By proposing Severa as the personification of both the Mouraria and the Fado, Dantas facilitates passive national curiosity about the theretofore deplorable Lisbon quarter; national sympathy toward the remarkable singer connotes consequent sympathy toward the Mouraria and the Fado.

But why does the *fado novo* appropriate Dantas's literary fantasy to understand its own history? The Fado's status as a national expression, while popularly accepted, was met with intellectual protest. In 1909, António Arroio writes: "In my opinion, the Fado expresses the state of inertia and sentimental inferiority into which our country has been plummeting for years, and from which we must escape. Portugal is a moral invalid and the Fado a sufficient symptom for us to diagnose the disease."[51] Arroio believes that as long as the Portuguese sing the Fado "with cigarettes hanging from the corners of their lips, their eyes rolled back in their heads, and their bosoms exploding with passion," they will remain an inferior people, unable to understand the modernity of civilized nations.[52]

For aesthetic reasons, in 1929, Afonso Lopes Vieira opposes the Fado as a Portuguese anthem: "In no way do I consider the 'Fado' the national song. It is only Lisbon's song, clumsy yet often biting. The nation that adopts as its anthem a similar tune must be truly lost. The 'Fado' is the pitiful pride and joy of Lisbon—a lyrical embarrassment."[53] The *fado novo* tries to overcome the critical schism concerning the Fado's value for a Portuguese society by demonstrating that the song has a universal audience. The *fado choradinho* that characterized the poor urban *fadista* class, the plangent song that Luís Moita would call the "*canção de vencidos*" [song of the vanquished], recedes as the *fado novo* appeals to Dantas's benign romanticization of the degraded nineteenth-century Mouraria.

The lyricists exploit two stages in Dantas's fictionalization of Severa's life in their attempt to link Severa's Mouraria and the Fado to the Portuguese character to vindicate the song in the Portuguese collective conscience. Some verses of the *fado novo* of the 1930s to 1970s attribute the origins of the Fado to the union between the disparate classes of the nobleman and the prostitute. Others support the Fado's candidacy for national song by marginalizing the deplored *fado chora-*

dinho to the poor urban quarters, by signaling the dissolution of the relationship between Severa and the Count as the birth of the Mouraria Fado.

Many Fados of the twentieth century refer to Dantas's interpretation of the romance between Severa and the Count of Vimioso / Marialva to appeal to a national audience by defending the Fado as good taste, thus reinvigorating Avelino de Sousa's 1912 support of the Fado as the national song: "Who cares if the ruffian or the whore mutilates the Fado? What does that prove? Simply that that beautiful song is in the soul of the people, and that precisely because it is sung by the lowest and the highest members on the social ladder, it has the status of a national song."[54] By reiterating the social disparity of Dantas's literary lovers, the Fado indicates its universal appeal in an attempt to promote its identity as a Portuguese anthem.

"Ah, Fado dum Ladrão" alludes to the nineteenth-century noblemen's predilection for the Mouraria prostitutes:

Todos dizem mal do fado
Mas dizer mal foi sempre moda
Pois ele já é cantado
Por gente de alta roda.[55]

[Everyone speaks ill of the Fado
But speaking ill of it was always in fashion
Yet the Fado is sung
By high society.]

The song reminds the Fado's detractors of the noblemen who visited the Mouraria to hear Severa:

Noutro tempo a fidalguia
Dava-se ao luxo ditoso era
De passar na Mouraria
As noites com a Severa.[56]

[In days gone by the nobility
Took pleasure in the luxury
Of coming to the Mouraria
To spend the night with Severa.]

It suggests an inherent Portuguese aesthetics of the Fado: "Ouvir dizer mal do que é nosso / Não é um bom português" [A real Portuguese / Would not allow others to speak ill of what is ours].

In a similar manner, "Anda Comigo," is an apology of the Fado as a Portuguese tradition that pervades all classes.[57] A *fadista* invites a friend to visit the Mouraria to hear Fado: "Anda comigo / Porque vais gostar deveras" [Come with me / Because you are really going to enjoy yourself]. The singer reminds his guest of the custom of the nobility's mingling with the lower classes, giving the example of Dantas's characters: "Por aqui também andaram / Marialvas e Severas" [Marialvas and Severas / Also were here]. He suggests that they continue the tradition:

> Veste a samarra
> Põe o teu chapéu de lado
> Traz contigo uma guitarra
> E vamos cantar o fado.
>
> [Put on your vest
> Tilt your hat to the side
> Bring your Portuguese guitar
> We are going to sing the Fado.]

They will reflect on their perpetuation of not only urban, but also national folklore: "Depois dirás mais uma vez / Como isto é bom e português" [Later you will remark / How good and Portuguese it is].

While many Fados view the birth of the national song as the fruit of a union between *fidalgo* and prostitute, "Tia Macheta" attributes the origins of the sad Mouraria Fado to the dissolution of that very relationship.[58] The sentimental *fado choradinho* of the degraded Mouraria, which Lopes Vieira and Arroio reject as a mere urban expression, ill-suited for national heritage, is relegated to the status of Lisbon's song: a song that does not appeal to all classes or to all regions. By exiling the Mouraria Fado from the canons of national songs, the lyrics of "Tia Macheta" support the *fado castiço* as a national expression.

Who was Tia Macheta?

Dantas created the character of Tia Macheta—a mixture of go-between, busybody and know-it-all—for his novel; however, the character did not appear in his play. Dantas's Macheta advises Severa's mother, Cesária/Barbuda, arranges a canon as her paramour, and intervenes to help keep young Severa in boarding school at the Coleginho. When Severa is an adult, Macheta brings Barbuda the news that her daughter is the Count of Marialva's lover. And toward the end of the novel, Macheta advises Severa, after she has rejected the Count.

In the Fado, Severa seeks counsel from Dantas's novelistic clairvoyant go-between, when the Count has disappeared:

O amante não aparecera
A triste Severa sempre fiel
Chamou a Tia Macheta
Velha alcoveta pra saber dele.

[When her love had not returned
Sad Severa, always loyal
Called on the old go-between, Tia Macheta
To find out what had become of him.]

Tia Macheta reads Severa's cards:

A velha pegou nas cartas
Sebentas fartas de mãos tão sujas
E antes de as embaralhar
Pôs-se a grasnar como as corujas.

[The old woman picked up some cards
Covered with the grease from her filthy hands
And before she shuffled them
She had begun to crow.]

Macheta's hand reveals Severa's fate: "'Ele não vem minha filha' / Tirou a espadilha de maus agoiros" ["He is not going to return, my child" / She drew the ace of spades from the deck], and implies that the Count has abandoned Severa for a noble woman: "'Há também uma viagem / Um personagem e a dama d'oiros'" ["I see a trip / An important person and the queen of diamonds"].[59] Severa waits for the Count until morning. When he does not return, the sad Fado of the Mouraria is born:

O fidalgo não voltou
Severa esperou até ser dia
E desde essa noite aqui existe
O fado triste da Mouraria.

[The Count never returned
Severa waited until dawn
Ever since that night
We sing the sad Mouraria Fado.]

The context of "Tia Macheta" remits us to a scene in Dantas's play that reiterates the *fado novo*'s and Avelino de Sousa's discourse concerning the national song: its appeal to all classes in Portuguese society. When the Count of Marialva locks Severa in his apartment so that she may not associate with the *fadistas* of the Bairro Alto and the Mouraria, he appropriates the Fado for the aristocracy by stealing it from the poor. By imprisoning the *fadista*, and allowing her to sing only with piano in salons, Marialva attempts to elevate the Fado as an elite song. But, the Mouraria Fado is, as Pimentel narrates: "A 'national anthem' . . . For the *fadista*, citizen of the infamous popular quarters, frequent visitor of dens of iniquity and bordellos, the entire country is summed up in that world, which is his 'fatherland,' his habitat."[60] Severa escapes through a window by jumping into a passing laundry wagon. She narrates to Timpanas: "The count locked me up in his house, on the second floor. I couldn't take it anymore! I went over to the window, where a washerwoman's wagon was passing, and I jumped into the piles of clothes!"[61]

Both Pinto de Carvalho and Pimentel believe that Dantas's scene of Severa's flight in a laundry wagon is adapted from a true story. Dantas may have written the episode of Severa's escape based on Pimentel's article from the *Diário de Notícias* (June 12, 1893), based on stories that he had gathered from the oral tradition. Pimentel reproduces the article in his book, in which he narrates the search for Severa. He tells us that one of the Count of Vimioso's friends found the *fadista* in a tavern on Travessa dos Inglesinhos in the Bairro Alto, where she was playing the Portuguese guitar, surrounded by an audience. The Count's friend peeked into the tavern and sang:

Todos aquelles que são
Da nossa sucia effectiva
Lamentam a fugitiva
Da Rua do Capellão.[62]

[Everybody who belongs
To our little crowd
Laments the flight of the fugitive
Of Rua do Capelão.]

Pimentel continues: "Severa, challenged, lifted up her head, as she had recognized that voice. She was trapped, she had been found, she felt like she had lost her freedom at that moment."[63]

Pinto de Carvalho attributes Severa's fleeing to the *fadista*'s boredom and nostalgia for the milieu of her class.[64] Pimentel suggests that Severa feared that the Count of Vimioso would lose interest in the affair: "She would prefer to spend her whole life eating grilled sardines than to enjoy *foie gras* for only one hour."[65] I believe that both arguments serve Dantas's propagandistic designs on the Fado as a national song. Pimentel notes: "[The *fadista*] is flattered by the higher classes' playing the Fado on the piano in sumptuous salons; like a foreigner who may feel flattered by hearing his nation's anthem appreciated in a land that is not his own."[66] Besides being a prisoner of the Count, Severa was an exile in a foreign land; Severa did not want to sing only for the elite, but for the variety of classes that constituted her audience in the Bairro Alto and the Mouraria.

In Dantas's novel, Severa explains to Macheta her motives for having left the Count: "If I wanted to, I'd return. But I don't want to. . . . I can't! I'm not willing give up my freedom for anyone. I love the sun, my independence, making my own decisions, without being anyone's captive, without owing anyone favors, free like the wind, being able to love whom I want, laughing and crying when I please. . . . Because life is just that!—Oh! But I really love him, Tia Macheta!"[67] In his play, Severa confronts Marialva:

> Well there you have it, prisons don't suit me! I love the sun, feasting, fasting, one day everything, the next day nothing, being free like the wind, wearing out my laughter as if it were a slipper, calling the world mine, paying tribute to nobody, and on every corner, showing off my red handkerchief and my freedom! If that's how you want me, so be it; if you don't want me, no problem! There's a lot of gold in the world; but just one Severa.[68]

In the following act, after Severa has not seen Marialva, she reads her own cards. Her fortune reveals that the Count will return.[69] The Fado "Tia Macheta," Severa's biography, and Dantas's novel, however, concur that the Count and the *fadista* do not reunite. Nevertheless, Dantas's dramatic Count returns. And his heroine dies beside him as she sings her final Fado.[70]

Júlio Dantas created the folkloric figure of the Mouraria *fadista* / prostitute in his fictionalization of Maria Severa's biography, rooted in a pastiche of historical and eyewitness accounts about the singer. Dantas's literary character would serve as the mold for later representations of Severa and of archetypal female *fadistas* of Lisbon's riverside. Furthermore, because the author's recreation of the nineteenth-century *fadista* quarter—in particular, Rua do Capelão—is the nation's first literary rendering of that Mouraria, and because Dantas collaborated on Leitão de Barros's cinematic portrayal of Rua do Capelão, his folkloric image of the Mouraria remains in the Portuguese collective conscience.

As Leitão de Barros's *A Severa* debuts alongside the CML's groundbreaking of its demolition of the Mouraria in the early 1930s, the Fado benefits to rewrite its own history and the Mouraria's recent history in the haze of Dantas's and Leitão de Barros's distorted memories. The Estado Novo profits from the Fado's promotion of a traditional Mouraria, despite the regime's eradication of that very quarter in the name of progress. Nevertheless, later *fado novo* lyricists will exploit Dantas's and Leitão de Barros's images of a traditional Mouraria to criticize the Estado Novo's destructive notion of progress. The *fadistas* and songwriters perpetuate the sympathetic literary and filmic treatments of the Mouraria, as they link the quarter to the national psyche by demonstrating the song's universality in its popularity among all strata of society. While the Fado is ridiculed as a Portuguese anthem in the late nineteenth century, the popular rewriting of Dantas's and Leitão de Barros's *A Severa*, cements the Fado's status as the national song.

2

Severa's Death and the Death of the *Fadista* Mouraria in the "Salvação Barreto" Demolitions

> The decadent races show great compassion toward figures who are incarnations of the soul of the people, who are their voice, their tears, the living representation of their traditions, the concrete form of their emotions.
>
> —Júlio Dantas

WHEREAS THE SOCIAL IMPOSSIBILITY OF AN AMOROUS RELATIONSHIP between Dantas's Count of Marialva and Severa may have flamed their passion, the same disparity of class complicated, and eventually dissolved, whatever romance there had been between the thirteenth Count of Vimioso and Maria Severa Onofriana. While Vimioso brought Severa to his palace to entertain his guests, and when he was seen playing the Portuguese guitar with the *fadista* at the bullring in Campo Pequeno, often Severa had to downplay her eccentricities to be accepted marginally in the dying aristocratic society. She was, after all, a novelty: an ostentatious decoration that was testimony to the aristocrat's daring, machismo, and apparent disregard of the social norms of a pre-Republican Lisbon. The Count of Vimioso's semiclandestine visits to Rua do Capelão were incongruous to a man of his social rank. He was an intriguing figure whose womanizing combined with his brio in the arena attested to his prowess, as he stood apart from other noblemen by following in the footsteps of the late eighteenth-century toreador, the Marquis of Marialva.[1]

Severa and Vimioso were characters from different worlds that coexisted, almost accidentally, in the same city during the same century. And although these worlds collided, from time to time, in the brothels of the Mouraria—a spatiotemporal sphere autonomous from that Romantic nineteenth-century Lisbon catalogued in history and literature—Severa and Vimioso were not involved in a legitimate relationship outside of the privileged locus of Lisbon's most sordid quarter.

Pinto de Carvalho's Dantas-inspired accounts of the star-crossed lovers whose kisses were merely "the Portuguese guitar's prelude to the ferocious chords of their embrace," have been refuted.[2] Sousa e Costa believes that Severa was in love with the abusive Count, whom he describes as distracted, impertinent, authoritarian, and even despotic.[3] Pimentel believes that the Count was, among gentlemen, a free-spirited bohemian but that he never degraded himself by falling in love with the prostitute. Furthermore, he believes that Severa never deluded herself into believing that their relationship amounted to more than a flight of fancy.[4] While Sucena does not believe that the affair was as cynical as Sousa e Costa and Pimentel say, he indicates that the Count replaced Severa with a new lover shortly after their breakup.[5] And Osório reminds us that despite Dantas's legend, Vimioso was a *marialva* and Severa a prostitute, therefore we would be naïve to believe that their love excluded others.[6]

Nevertheless, Dantas's fictionalized union between the lowest urban class and nobility in Severa and Marialva's romance—and the alluded romance between the singer and Vimioso—represents something much more important than the historical details of their affair; it signals the democratization of Lisbon's folkloric aesthetics in the Fado, a necessary step in the nationalization of the urban song. Avelino de Sousa's argument (1912) that the Fado is a national song because it appeals to all classes in Portuguese society reflects and even defends Dantas's characterization of the aristocrat, Marialva, who is devastated by the news of the prostitute/*fadista*'s death. In the final pages of Dantas's drama and novel, we observe a Lisbon—noble, bourgeois, holy, and untouchable—crying for the *fadista*'s soul. In her death, Severa transcends class: she is mourned by *fadistas* and nobility alike; she transcends her profession and is remembered more as a *fadista* than as a prostitute. She also transcends the Mouraria: she brings the Fado out of the popular neighborhood into noble salons. Severa becomes a Portuguese icon and, through her death, her Fado is mourned as a national song. In the last pages of his novel, Dantas comments, "when the Gypsy harlot died, a bit of the Portuguese soul died with her."[7] For the first time since Camões's death in 1580, in the same miserable neighborhood, Portugal's lyrical tradition is linked to the Mouraria.

The *fado novo* of the mid to late twentieth century preserves Dantas's historical fiction in its memory of Severa's death. One legend resembles the end of Dantas's drama in which Severa dies beside the Count or in his arms:

Àquela hora
Nos braços do seu amado
Cantava agora
O seu derradeiro fado.[8]

[At that moment
In the arms of her lover
She sang
Her final Fado.]

The other elaborates on the last pages of Dantas's novel, in which a grieving Custódia brings Marialva the news of Severa's death:

O Conde de Vimioso
Um duro golpe sofreu
Quando lhe foram dizer
"Tua Severa morreu."[9]

[The Count of Vimioso
Suffered a hard blow
When they told him
"Your Severa is dead."]

Dantas's mise en scène of Severa's agony, in the presence of the Fado, and the Mouraria *fadista* singing spontaneously Sousa do Casacão's "Fado da Severa," has promoted the Fado's association as the national song:

Chorem, chorem os fadistas
E chore toda a nação
Morreu a Severa, a flor
Da Rua do Capelão![10]

[Cry, cry *fadistas*
And cry everyone in the nation

Severa, the flower of Rua do Capelão
Is dead.]

Sousa do Casacão's lyrics, which serve to announce Severa's death in Dantas's play and novel, constitute a criticism of the Estado Novo and the CML in the *fado novo* of the 1930s to 1970s. The *fado novo* criticizes the antihistorical venture of urban modernization by calling the public's attention to the destruction of the Fado's patrimony. What might appear to be a cause of interest to residents of the Mouraria or, perhaps, architectural conservationists in Lisbon, becomes relevant to a nation, thanks to the Fado and to Dantas's cultivation of an inextricable correlation between the national song and the endangered quarter. The *fadista* does not bemoan simply the death of a singer; rather, he mourns the death of the national song as a consequence of the death of the Mouraria in the twentieth-century rehabilitation of Lisbon's riverside. As a result, *fado novo* lyricists of the 1930s to 1970s have elevated the urban song in the national psyche by recycling Dantas's dramatization/novelization of Severa's life and death as relevant to Portuguese outside of Lisbon. Sousa do Casacão's refrain from the "Fado da Severa" is recontextualized in the *fado novo* to draw the nation's attention to the imminent death of the Fado, or rather, the death of Portugal's national song, in the modernization of Lisbon's Mouraria.

Eduardo Faria's 1952 cartoon, "Fado da Demolição" [Fado of the Demolition] is evidence of the relevance of Sousa do Casacão's lyrics as criticism of the "Salvação Barreto" program. His drawing depicts a crying nineteenth-century *fadista* who wanders through the rubble of the twentieth-century Baixa Mouraria, as he sings to the tune of the "Fado da Severa":

Chorai, fadistas, chorai
Que a Mouraria lá vai
E está quase no 'squeleto
Apesar da tradição
É bairro sem salvação
Com o Salvação Barreto.[11]

[Cry, *fadistas*, cry
There goes the Mouraria
It's a mere skeleton
Despite tradition

It's a quarter without salvation
With the "Salvação Barreto" program.]

Faria's cartoon reappropriates Dantas's appropriation of Sousa do Casacão's Fado to view Severa's death as the death of the Mouraria and the death of Portuguese traditions in the Estado Novo's obsession with architectural progress. As Lisbon tradition cedes to the Estado Novo's ostensible modernization, the *fado novo* reestablishes its folkloric link to Dantas's and Leitão de Barros's Mouraria. The *fado novo*, thus, expresses its unconditional protest to the Mouraria's demolition; Severa's Mouraria represents the Fado's golden age, and the Estado Novo's modernization proposes to eradicate all architectural vestiges of the Fado's heritage. The regime's contradictory discourses of progress and tradition are exposed when the *fado novo* proves, with the living/dying example of the Mouraria, that one ideology must yield to the other. The envisioned new Mouraria is a sterile shell of Severa's Mouraria, a "mere skeleton," devoid of Portuguese tradition and alien to the Fado. And the crying pre-Republican *fadista*, in bell-bottom trousers and with a cigarette hanging from his lip, personifies that Mouraria, as he makes his exodus from his ravaged home. He is folklore displaced by the cold, modernizing aesthetics of a merciless regime!

Portuguese readers in the 1950s understand the humor of Faria's cartoon for three reasons. The first is the popularity of Sousa do Casacão's lyrics that by the late nineteenth century were known in one form or another by almost everybody in Portugal:

Chorai, fadistas, chorai
Que a Severa morreu
Fadistas como ela
O fado nunca conheceu.[12]

[Cry, *fadistas*, cry
For Severa is dead
Fadistas like Severa
The Fado has never known.]

The second is Dantas's and, later, Leitão de Barros's recontextualization of Sousa do Casacão's lyrics following their heroine's death scene. Fifty years after Sousa do Casacão had written the prostitute's eulogy, Dantas would reiterate the association between Severa, the Mouraria, and the Fado to indicate the death of Portugal's pre-Republican traditions in the *fadista*'s death. And finally, we have the *fado novo*'s perpetuation of Sousa do Casacão's lyrics: a legacy received directly in the 1930s, not from the nineteenth-century lyricist, but rather from Dantas and Leitão de Barros's reevaluation of the song's verses to reiterate that indeed, a bit of Portugal's soul died with that gypsy harlot.[13]

Dantas convinces his audience of the association between Severa, the Mouraria, and the Fado, when his protagonist brags: "I am the Mouraria . . . I am the Fado!"[14] And he later establishes a relationship between the Fado and the Portuguese national character when a teary Count of Marialva hands Severa a Portuguese guitar and declares: "It is Portugal's destiny to die in the arms of the Fado."[15] In Leitão de Barros's film, Severa echoes Marialva's lines in verse:

Tenho o destino marcado
Desde a hora em que te vi
Ó meu cigano adorado
Viver abraçada ao fado
Morrer abraçada a ti.[16]

[My fate has been sealed
Since the moment that I saw you
Oh, my beloved Gypsy
To live in the arms of the Fado
And to die in your arms.]

Dantas's formula concludes that if Severa is the Mouraria, if she is the Fado, and if she shares Portugal's fate to [live and] die in the Fado's arms, then she also must be Portugal. Within the context of Dantas's four-act play, Severa's fatal collapse while singing the national song is significant; the theatrical Severa realizes Portugal's destiny to die embracing the Fado. The *fadista* is transformed through her agony; she is no longer a miserable prostitute on Rua do Capelão, nor is she a mere icon of the Mouraria, or even Lisbon; rather, Severa reenacts the death of all Portuguese in her final Fado: a national song. Thus, Dantas's characterization of Severa exceeds the local boundaries of the Mouraria and the unfortunate consequences of the *fadista*'s life to propose the singing prostitute as an emblem of the Portuguese people. In his proposal, Dantas, perhaps unwittingly, cultivates a sympathetic relationship between the nation and the Mouraria. And the *fado novo*'s lyricists profit seemingly from Dantas's metaphor.

The circumstances of Severa's death, however, were quite different than Dantas's protagonist's Romantic fainting spell in the ecstasy of her Fado. Pimentel and Araújo believe that the *fadista* died of indigestion: an echo of the legend that the prostitute choked to death on her own vomit during a meal of pigeon and wine. Pinto de Carvalho believes that Severa died in a hospital bed of complications related to syphilis—conjecture based on her social status as a streetwalker—or tuberculosis, consistent with the *fadista*'s image as a pathetic, Romantic figure: Portugal's *Lady of the Camellias.*[17] According to Severa's burial record, she died at 9:00 p.m. on November 30, 1846. Her death certificate, issued November 16, 1848, and her burial record at the Alto de São João Cemetery in the Socorro Parish, report apoplexy as her cause of death.[18] However, Sousa e Costa refutes these documents by citing an interview with the military doctor who had examined the *fadista* in 1846, who confirmed that Severa had suffered from tachycardia, and that she had complained of pains consistent with angina in the left side of her chest.[19]

Sousa e Costa's biography of Severa intends to shed light on popular legends that circulated about the *fadista* since her death, by paraphrasing interviews with people who knew the *fadista* or who lived in the Mouraria in the 1840s. However, Sousa e Costa's book was published in 1936, five years after Leitão de Barros's *A Severa*, and therefore, the author's informants and the author may suffer from the cultural amnesia brought on by the recent filmic distortions of their own memories. Sousa e Costa's seemingly objective Severa of her neighbors' eyewitness accounts is, at times, as dramatic and even more Romantic than Dantas's and Leitão de Barros's literary and cinematic avatars. And while Sousa e Costa's Severa may not die, literally, in the Fado's embrace, every line that she utters in her last days appears to be a Fado or lost lines from Dantas's four-act play.

According to Sousa e Costa, those who were near Severa, during her agony, believe that she wanted to die: "I am dying without ever having lived . . . when will my time come?" the *fadista* complained, "it's taking forever for me to rest, once and for all!"[20] And the author quotes the following verses, attributed to a dying Severa:

Tenho a vida amargurada
Ai que destino infeliz
Mas se sou tão desgraçada
Não fui eu que assim quis![21]

[My life is embittered
Oh, what an unhappy fate
But if I am so disgraced
It wasn't my fault!]

Let us compare their tone and objective to César das Neves's "Canção da Desgraçada":

Quem tiver filhas no mundo
Não fale das desgraçadas
Porque as filhas da desgraça
Também nasceram honradas.[22]

[Anyone who has daughters in this world
Don't speak of disgraced women
Because the daughters of disgrace
Also were born honorable.]

And the real-life Severa's song: "Quando eu morrer não tenham pesar algum! / E ao som das vossas cantigas / Lancem-me à vala comum!" [When I die don't feel any sorrow / And to the tune of your songs / Throw me into the common grave!] resembles the suffering tone of Dantas's heroine's:

Tenho o destino marcado
Desde que a saia vesti
Eu quero morrer cantando
Já que chorando nasci.[23]

[My fate has been sealed
Ever since I put on my first skirt
I want to die singing
For I was born crying.]

While the goal of Sousa e Costa's book is to demystify Severa's legend, he perpetuates the very myths that he proposes to dispel. The influence of Sousa do Casacão's Fado, Dantas's novel and play, and Leitão de Barros's film are all too prevalent, and have managed to fictionalize the accounts of Severa's contemporaries. That Severa's life provoked more historical interest in the ninety years after the *fadista*'s death can be summed up in the hyperbolic propaganda of Sousa do

Casacão's eulogy, which urges not just the *fadistas* of the Mouraria, but the whole nation to cry for her soul.

In Pinto de Magalhães's cartoon, "Um Desastre. 'A Severa' . . . Já Morreu" [Disaster. "A Severa" . . . Is Dead], Sousa do Casacão's lyrics are parodied to demonstrate Dantas's and Leitão de Barros's grotesque disfiguration of the Severa myth. First, Magalhães reappropriates Sousa do Casacão's lyrics from Dantas's play to attack the very dramatic spectacle by its association with Leitão de Barros's cinematic rendering. Magalhães's caricature cannibalizes *A Severa*'s last lines as a means to mock Dantas's perpetuation of a decadent, romanticized legend. Secondly, within the cartoon's title is a play on both the lyrics of Sousa do Casacão's "Fado da Severa" and the title of Leitão de Barros's film (and Dantas's homonymous novel and play). Therefore, Magalhães's title announces not Severa's death—as did Sousa do Casacão's lyrics—rather, it proclaims the definitive death of hackneyed, performative interpretations of Severa's life, or Leitão de Barros's murdering (with the complicity of Dantas's artistic direction) of the Severa myth in his filmic adaptation of Dantas's play and novel.

Magalhães's cartoon depicts Dantas sitting on Severa's lap, playing a Portuguese guitar, while a nineteenth-century *fadista* covers his ears. Dantas collaborated on Leitão de Barros's film's soundtrack and wrote its most recognizable song, "Novo Fado da Severa (Rua do Capelão)," therefore he is the musician, or rather the Sousa do Casacão, behind *A Severa*. At the same time, the popular author is slave to his own larger-than-life Severa on whose lap he sits. However, Severa's contemporary, the Mouraria *fadista* in bell-bottom trousers, a figure who should venerate Severa, does not recognize her and rejects her new avatar by covering his ears.

The accompanying text—a criticism of the 1931 film—recycles Sousa do Casacão's refrain: "Now we can truly sing, with respect to the film: Cry, *fadistas*, cry—for Severa is dead . . . The hyped film, produced in Paris, is everything but Severa. Inferior in plot, inferior in production, inferior in every aspect. For two or three escudos, at a cheap movie theatre, it is tolerable. For much more than that, no way."[24] Although Magalhães may be correct in his criticism of Dantas's and Leitão de Barros's aesthetic death blow to Severa's biography, the cartoonist was not an astute prophet of trends in popular culture. I argue that Leitão de Barros's film signals not Severa's death, but rather her rebirth in Dina Teresa's rendition of "Novo Fado da Severa (Rua do Capelão)" and the consequent birth of the *fado novo* coetaneous to Lisbon's renaissance in the Estado Novo's modernization of the capital.[25]

I have noted that Teófilo Braga's publication of Sousa do Casacão's "Fado da Severa" has played a crucial role in the diffusion of the legend of the Mouraria *fadista.* The *fado novo* lyricists of the 1930s to 1970s reinterpret Sousa do Casacão's lament of Severa's death as the death of the Mouraria as the quarter yields to Lisbon's modernization, and as a new generation moves away from the Fado. Already in 1901, Dantas remarks: "[Severa] was the symbol of the old Fado that was disappearing."[26] Severa's death is the death of the Mouraria, and the consequent death of the Fado. In its reiteration of Dantas's proposal of Severa as an emblem of the Fado and the Mouraria, the *fado novo* announces the death of the national song and the destruction of the cradle of the national song in the Estado Novo's leveling of the Mouraria. As a consequence, the destiny of the Portuguese to die in the arms of the Fado is made impossible by the progressive extinction of the song, as a result of the architectural death of the Mouraria and the changing values of the Portuguese who shun the Fado as an outdated genre.

Dantas's insistence on Severa as the incarnation of Portugal, an avatar who shares the country's fate to die in the Fado's arms, is central to the Fado lyricists' denunciation of the CML's demolition of the Mouraria, as Dantas's literary character is responsible for having made the disappearing neighborhood relevant to Portuguese outside of Lisbon. By linking Severa's death to the death of the Fado, and by recontextualizing Sousa do Casacão's "Fado da Severa" for an audience growing alien to the Fado during Lisbon's inevitable modernization, the *fado novo* appeals to a national audience. The lyricists call the public's attention to its apparently small-scale, local criticism of the Estado Novo at the moment when the Fado becomes the privileged song of the regime, through the 1933 launching of the Emissora Nacional: the official radio station of the Estado Novo's propaganda.[27]

António Porto accuses the Estado Novo of having exploited Fado broadcasts on the Emissora Nacional to cultivate national curiosity surrounding the Fado as a means to orient the nation's popular culture toward Lisbon:

> Lisbon's bureaucracy, in an attempt to defuse certain Northern resistance to the regime and to its center [in the capital], broadcasted on radio and television, massive doses of Lisbon Fado and the situation got to the point

> that, even in Oporto, one was not considered Portuguese if he/she did not go at least once in his/her life, not to Mecca but to the Mouraria or Alfama, to hear a quaint, tear-jerking Fado session, worthy of our national disgrace, dating back to [the Battle of] Alcácer-Quibir, where, according to some sources, ten thousand Portuguese guitars were recovered after the tragic defeat.[28]

However, before Portugal went to the cinema to hear Dina Teresa sing, as Severa, in Leitão de Barros's film, before Luís Moita's eight-episode radio tirade against the Fado's status as a national song, *O Fado, Canção de Vencidos* (1936), and before the SPN realized that it could harness the Fado's popularity to promote the Estado Novo's propaganda, the Fado had become the national song.

In 1888, Eça de Queiroz's character, Ega had called the Fado, "our great national invention."[29] In 1917, José Malhoa's painting, *O Fado* had been displayed at the Sociedade Nacional de Belas-Artes in Lisbon: a testimony to the popularity of the song among all classes in Portuguese society. In 1923, French filmmaker Maurice Mariaud had chosen to adapt Bento Mântua's play about Malhoa's painting, as Caldelvilla Film's first production, during a period when Portuguese cinema was dominated by adaptations of the cornerstones of national literature. Ventura de Abrantes had called the Fado, "the most Portuguese of all songs" and "the liturgy of the Portuguese soul, the nation's soul."[30] And, in 1929, ethnomusicologist Rodney Gallop had gone to the remote Trás-os-Montes region, hoping to hear local songs; instead, he heard a washerwoman's rendition of a Mouraria Fado.

Even though Porto is correct to attribute the massive diffusion of the Fado to the inception of the Emissora Nacional in the 1930s—and the national televised broadcasts of Fado performances in the late 1950s—he ignores that the Fado had earned the reputation, however controversial, of national song before the existence of the Estado Novo. Nevertheless, I would like to signal in Porto's accusation the metaphor of the Mouraria and Alfama as Mecca: historical, however, propagandistic epicenters of Fado, de rigueur for any true Portuguese. The metaphor implies that the regime exploited these sacred spaces through radio broadcast to make Lisbon the nucleus of the Estado Novo's notion of Portuguese identity. Thus, Porto's argument reasons that the Estado Novo was complicit with the *fado novo*'s marketing of the Mouraria and Alfama as emblematic Portuguese neighborhoods; for that reason, neighborhoods that should be protected as part of a national heritage. The *fado novo* wields tradition as a subversive discourse to attack the Estado Novo's destructive discourse of progress; yet the regime appropriates the *fado novo*'s criticism of Lisbon's modernization to portray a false image of the capital. By promoting the artificial memory of the Mouraria that they have destroyed and continue to destroy single-handedly, the Estado Novo profits from the *fado novo*'s critical discourse, and thus disarms it by not censoring it. The Estado Novo seems to have its cake and eat it: while tradition must give way to progress, in the Mouraria, memory and nostalgia allow us to honor tradition and keep it alive despite its material annihilation.

The song, "Mataram a Mouraria" questions the relationship between tradition and progress as it personifies the Fado's mourning the murder of the Mouraria:

> Já tarde quando passava
> Ouvi alguém a gemer
> Naquela rua sombria
> Era o fado que chorava
> Porque lhe foram dizer
> Mataram a Mouraria.[31]
>
> [It was late when it happened
> I heard somebody moaning
> On that somber street
> It was the Fado who was crying
> Because they had come to tell him
> That they had killed the Mouraria.]

At first glance, the lyrics valiantly assign blame to the "Salvação Barreto" rehabilitation projects for the Mouraria's architectural homicide. Nevertheless, the personification of tradition tries to console the Fado with the pragmatism of experience:

> A tradição condoída
> Também chorava por ver
> O amigo desolado
> E dizia "é lei da vida
> Vem o futuro nascer
> E vai morrendo o passado."

[Compassionate tradition
Also cried
When she saw her afflicted friend
And she said "it's just life
The future is born
As the past dies."]

The Fado, however, senses his own alienation and consequent mortality in the murder of the Mouraria:

O fado já mal se ouvia
Mas teve forças ainda
Pra dizer à companheira
"Mataram a Mouraria
Velhinha que foi tão linda
Já não tenho quem me queira."

[The Fado could hardly speak
But he mustered up energy
To say to his friend
"They killed the Mouraria
That beautiful old lady
Now nobody loves me."]

The Fado's final verse, however, tempers the lyrics' aggression toward the "Salvação Barreto" program—and by association, the Estado Novo—by questioning the *fado novo*'s tendency to equate progress with the loss of tradition: "Enquanto houver portugueses / Ninguém diga em Portugal / Que vai morrendo o passado" [As long as there are Portuguese people / Don't tell me that / Tradition is dying in Portugal]. By viewing tradition not in material, but in abstract terms, "Mataram a Mouraria" puts the onus on the Portuguese to maintain their historical conscience, despite the demolitions. And, as this advice is uttered by the Fado, the song's lyricist betrays the criticism of the first three verses to exonerate the murderers with the empty notion that progress and tradition can coexist, even when all concrete vestiges of tradition have yielded to that progress.

Perhaps the Estado Novo's consenting to the *fado novo*'s memory of tradition has allowed the song to thrive despite its subversive criticism of the regime. The Estado Novo fosters an aesthetics of modernization—tangible in its demolition of a decayed historical Lisbon and rebuilding of monolithic white apartment complexes—as it simultaneously adheres to and sustains an oppressive memory of history. The *fado novo* aims tradition at the regime, using it as a weapon to attack the Estado Novo's/CML's demolition projects by exposing the anti-historical nature of a discourse of modernity. Nevertheless, the Estado Novo's Janus-faced philosophy allows it to benefit from a combination of material, architectural progress and abstract, yet ever-conscious nostalgia. Thus the regime absorbs the *fado novo*'s discourse of tradition as it promotes the memory of Lisbon's riverside, marketed as sanitized folkloric nostalgia, as it abandons conservancy of the area's architecture.

I have discussed earlier the Estado Novo's wholesale sanitization of the Mouraria as the quintessential artificial folkloric Lisbon neighborhood, by its association with Alfama, in Perdigão Queiroga's film, *Fado, História d'uma Cantadeira* (1947). I remarked that the Ministry of Public Works had planned to bring progress to Alfama, once it had leveled the Mouraria. Nevertheless, the trends in urban rehabilitation had moved away from demolition and toward preservation before the CML could get its hands on Alfama. In Queiroga's movie, the polemic concerning the contradictory discourses of tradition and progress is evident in the chatter of the producers and critics (Reginaldo Duarte and José Zenóglio) as they consider how they will market Alfama *fadista*, Ana Maria's (Amália Rodrigues) image. Producer, Sousa Morais (Tony D'Algy), suggests: "The typical background with the all the flavor of Alfama." They will take Alfama out of Alfama, yet they will preserve it as folklore, while exploiting popular memory. When the star debuts on stage, symbolically singing "Fado, Não Sei Quem És" [Fado, I Don't Know Who You Are], she steps out of a giant Portuguese guitar lodged in a theatrical recreation of Alfama: a cardboard reconstruction of the convergence of the Escadinhas de Santo Estêvão and Rua dos Remédios.[32] The stage set signals the artificial folklorization of that Alfama/Mouraria that must yield to progress: Alfamas and Mourarias destroyed and reborn, caricatured in the *fado novo*. The modernization of Lisbon will take the Fado with it and leave behind the *fado novo* and synthetic reproductions of a picturesque, *fadista* Alfama (or Mouraria), suitable for a tourist's tastes and convenient to the regime's otherwise irreconcilable tug of war between urban tradition and progress.[33]

The *fado novo's* lyricists recognize their collusion with the Estado Novo's betrayal of Lisbon's riverside. They become aware that the regime, and particularly the SNI, are the beneficiaries of their reconstruction of the lost Mouraria and the threatened Alfama. Perhaps only in retrospect, we observe Henrique Campos's film, *Rosa de Alfama* (1953), as Lisboa Filme's—and by association, the SNI's—most blatant example of artificial folklorization to the detriment of the Fado and the profit of the regime. The movie is a late, even passé manifestation of the *nacional-cançonetismo* style, a musical film genre that marketed neighborhood values to bourgeois urban audiences.[34] Lisbon's real riverside makes a brief appearance during the opening scene when a crooning Alberto Ribeiro approaches the Ribeira Velha. However, for the rest of the movie, we are stuck on a film set recreation of Alfama: much cleaner, and architecturally not quite Alfama. And the accompanying music, *fado canção*, only vaguely resembles nineteenth- or even early twentieth-century Fado. We are reminded of Sousa Morais's proposal in *Fado, História d'uma Cantadeira*, as we are left with the (bitter) flavor of a cardboard Alfama backdrop, and the indigestible *fado canção* that plagues Campos's film.

As the *fado novo* tires of its complicity with the Estado Novo's understanding of reconciliation between progress and tradition, the lyricists no longer recreate Severa's Mouraria for posterity; rather, they mourn Severa's death as they mourn the death of the Mouraria in the "Salvação Barreto" demolitions. By announcing and mourning the Mouraria's death, the *fado novo* halts its participation in a folkloric reconstruction of a lost Mouraria, as it criticizes the agents of the neighborhood's destruction. Therefore, the Estado Novo's aesthetic balance between progress and tradition is shrugged off as merely theoretical, as the Fado narrates Lisbon's loss, and denies the Mouraria's existence as anything but a distant memory.

The theme of Maria Severa's death—as allegory for the definitive death of the Mouraria in the "Salvação Barreto" program—appears repeatedly in the *fado novo* to undermine the Estado Novo's exploitation of the neighborhood's memory. By pronouncing the quarter's death, the *fadistas* manage to subvert the regime's appropriation of the Fado's artificial folklorization of the Mouraria. The broadcasted message no longer beckons Portuguese to make a patriotic pilgrimage to the symbolic neighborhood—as Porto argues; rather, it exposes the void behind the folkloric façade. As the SNI compensates its demolition of the Mouraria by promoting the memory of the quarter, the *fadistas* return to Dantas's equation: the death of Severa is the death of the Mouraria, the Fado, and Portugal's soul. The last lines of "Mataram a Mouraria," that insist that we view tradition in abstract terms are thrown out as the *fadista* argues that the material death of the Mouraria is the death of the neighborhood's soul.

"Fadista Louco" narrates the story of a mad singer who recalls Severa's Mouraria:

Falava na Amendoeira
Na Guia e no Capelão
Na Rosária e na Camiseira
E na Tasca do Gingão.[35]

[He spoke about Rua da Amendoeira
Rua da Guia and Rua do Capelão
The Rosária and Camiseira bars
And Gingão's pub.]

However, the first verse of the song decries the mad *fadista*'s lyrics as nonsense—babble unintelligible to those who listen:

Contaram-me ainda há pouco
Que à noite p'la Mouraria
Andava um fadista louco
Sem saber o que dizia.

[They told me a little while ago
That at night in the Mouraria
A madman wandered about
Without knowing what he was saying.]

The madman is part of incarnate Lisbon folklore who: "Cantava um fado velhinho / Dedilhando uma guitarra" [Sang an old Fado / As he strummed a Portuguese guitar]. But that folklore seems irrelevant as his words allude to a period that nobody understands. He moans for Severa's death, then disappears—a testament to his mere abstraction:

Louco gritou p'la Severa
E quando a manhã surgiu
Quando alguém quis ver quem era
Nunca mais ninguém o viu.

[The madman screamed for Severa
And when the morning came

Front door of Maria Severa's house on Rua do Capelão, photograph by Susana Correia.

When they tried to see who he was
Nobody could find him.]

And his apparent announcement of Severa's death turns out to be his mourning the death of the Mouraria in the "Salvação Barreto" demolitions:

Então fiquei meditando
Que o louco que ninguém via
Era a saudade chorando
A morte da Mouraria.

[So I started thinking
That the madman whom nobody could see
Was nostalgia's mourning
The death of the Mouraria.]

In this Fado, the madman is not the quaint folkloric type who coexists with the modern neighborhood and lends it local charm. Instead, he is a haunting figure: at once a reminder of tragedy and an outcast. He is inconvenient to a progressive Lisbon, and as he recalls the Mouraria's sacrifice, he is silenced, denied, forgotten.

The Fado "Pobre Bairro" also accuses the "Salvação Barreto" project of having destroyed the traditional Mouraria as it asks:

Mouraria, Mouraria
Meu berço, minha quimera!
Que fizeste da Severa
E dos fadistas que havia?[36]

[Mouraria, Mouraria
My crib, my fancy!
What have you done with Severa
And the *fadistas* who once lived there?]

By accusing the new, progressive Mouraria of having betrayed the native *fadistas*, "Pobre Bairro" undermines the Estado Novo's exploitation of the Mouraria's history. The Fado declares that the present Mouraria is not the *fadista* Mouraria that it was:

Meu pobre bairro, coitado
Perdeste toda a poesia

Já não és a Mouraria
És a sombra do passado.

[My poor, pitiable neighborhood
You lost all of your poetry
You are no longer the Mouraria
You are just a shadow of your past.]

If the postdemolition Mouraria should be a pilgrimage site for *fadistas*, it will only be so in their imagination. When the "true Portuguese" (to whom Porto alludes) obey the Emissora Nacional, and travel to the *fadista*'s Mecca, they will see the void, the mere "shadow of [the] past." The *fadista* turns his/her back to the modern Mouraria as he/she rejects complicity with the SNI's propaganda that promotes a traditional yet progressive riverside.

Nevertheless, as tradition's avatar in "Mataram a Mouraria" reminds us, Lisbon's modernization is inevitable, and the Fado's alienation, a consequence of the modern capital. The Fado links Severa's death to the death of the Fado by recontextualizing Sousa do Casacão's "Fado da Severa" for an audience moving away from the Fado during Lisbon's modernization. "Anda o Fado n'Outras Bocas" borrows the refrain from Sousa do Casacão's "Fado da Severa," "Chorai, fadistas chorai / Como dizia a cantiga" [Cry, *fadistas* cry / Just like the old song used to say], to comment on the Fado's absence from a new Mouraria without traditions. The lyrics expose the impossibility of a traditional Lisbon within the Estado Novo's/CML's plans for the Mouraria's progress:

Andei p'la Mouraria
Nas tascas d'antigamente
Mas o fado estava ausente
Mudou de lá quem diria?[37]

[I wandered the Mouraria
In all of the pubs of yore
But the Fado was gone
It had moved away, who would have guessed?]

The Fado has been distorted by a generation that does not understand Severa's Mouraria, because it cannot. The nineteenth-century Mouraria becomes more distant as memory distorts it, and real traditions suffer:

Cantai, fadistas cantai
Com vossas gargantas roucas
Que anda o fado n'outras bocas
Que não são bocas prò fado.[38]

[Sing, *fadistas* sing
With your hoarse voices
For the Fado dwells in new mouths
That aren't meant for the Fado.]

And this Fado predicts that without the Mouraria, the Fado soon will be extinct.

In a similar manner, the Fado "Maria Severa" remarks on the absence of tradition in the endangered Mouraria, by posing the question of what will become of the abandoned Fado: "Que vai ser desse enjeitado / Se perdeu o maior bem / O amor da mãe" [What will happen to that orphan / If he has lost his greatest treasure / His mother's love]. Rather, what will happen to the Fado when the Mouraria has disappeared? And the singer resigns to accept his/her role as part of the last generation of Mouraria *fadistas*, by alluding to Sousa do Casacão's Fado in his/her refrain: "Fadistas chorai / Porque ela morreu" [*Fadistas* cry / Because [Severa] is dead]. Thus the Fado "Maria Severa" perpetuates Dantas's association between Severa's death, the death of the Mouraria, and the death of the Fado, to blame the regime for the loss of tradition, a consequence of the annihilating progress.

Dantas's representation of Severa's death, in his novel and in his play, followed by the refrain from Sousa do Casacão's "Fado da Severa" has made an impact on the *fado novo* of the 1930s to 1970s by presenting the *fadista*'s death as a national concern. Dantas identifies the *fadista* as a national figure, because of her association with the national song, and thus he has made the Mouraria relevant to Portuguese outside of Lisbon. *Fado novo* lyricists have benefited from Dantas's proposal of Severa as a national figure to draw the nation's attention to the historical importance of the Mouraria by way of its association with the national song. In the *fado novo* of the 1930s to 1970s, Severa's death and Sousa do Casacão's eulogy of the singer are recontextualized to criticize the Estado Novo's demolition of the Mouraria by accusing the regime of destroying national folkloric tradition in its demolition of the poetic birthplace of the national song.

The *fado novo* exploits the Estado Novo's contradictory discourses of progress and tradition to prove, with the example of the leveling of the Mouraria, that the loss of tradition and a national heritage are the price that we must pay for the modernization of Lisbon. The *fado novo* first orchestrates its attack against Lisbon's antihistorical renovation at the moment when the Fado becomes the consecrated song of the regime, through the launching of the Emissora Nacional, the radio station of the regime's propaganda. While the Fado was already recognized, embraced, and refuted as the national song, the Fado's national diffusion—through radio, and later, television broadcasts cemented the song's central role as the soundtrack for the Estado Novo.

Whereas the *fado novo* uses tradition to attack the Estado Novo's plan for progress, the regime benefits from such an attack. The SNI promotes the *fado novo*'s concept of progress by exploiting the memory of the Mouraria that they have destroyed. The Estado Novo argues that the Portuguese must maintain a sense of national traditions by honoring the memory of Lisbon's riverside, although the material evidence of such a history may have been demolished. The *fado novo* launches a counterattack on the regime's appropriation of their notion of urban and national traditions by announcing the death of the Mouraria, the national song, and Portuguese traditions in the destruction of the Mouraria. In the *fado novo*'s scheme, Severa's death and Sousa do Casacão's eulogy of her death are recontextualized to expose the Estado Novo's fallacy that tradition and progress can coexist, when such progress implies the erasing of the material vestiges of Portuguese history.

3

The Reconstruction of a Mouraria of Contrasts: The Aristocratic and *Fadista* Mourarias and Reincarnations of Severa and Marialva

> The nobleman who did not want to cause a scene and have to confront the jealous fury of the noble lady made the trip [from the São Carlos Opera House to Calçada de Carriche] in modest, beaten-up carriages, less comfortable, but a lot more fun! The bohemian caravan was not limited to the foreign beauties escorted by elegant gentlemen. It included the cream of the *fadista* circles: Cesária, Severa, Maria Vitória and Júlia Mendes, whose satin slippers have left their footprints on the cobblestones in these parts.
>
> —Beatriz Costa

DANTAS'S AND LEITÃO DE BARROS'S TWENTIETH-CENTURY VISIONS of a pre-Republican Mouraria, in which aristocrats socialize with *fadistas*, reflect a nineteenth-century urban phenomenon: a Lisbon in which diverse social groups share popular neighborhoods. The proximity of the aristocratic Mouraria of the Palaces of the Marquis of Alegrete and the Marquis of Ponte de Lima (Palácio da Rosa) to the *fadista* quarter of Rua do Capelão and Rua da Amendoeira is architectural testimony of cohabitation between distant social classes. Duarte Pacheco's and Faria da Costa's utopian housing projects that sought to force the bourgeoisie to share rehabilitated neighborhoods with the poor—thus replicating the Mouraria's social reality in the nineteenth century—did not justify the demolition of the Mouraria in the name of social progress.

In terms of architecture, the Mouraria of the nineteenth century already was a theatre of social contrasts. Thus the CML vindicated the Estado Novo's support of the demolition of Lisbon's historic riverside by defining its notion of progress in relation to hygiene. In the late 1920s and early 1930s the CML was trying to shake Lisbon's image as Portugal's dirty, abandoned capital.[1] As the Mouraria had been a neighborhood on the margins of Lisbon's consensual notion of morality since well before the Liberal Regime of 1833, it was an easy target for the Estado Novo's progress. Norberto de Araújo suggests that should we eradicate the *fadista* Mouraria, in the name of sanitation and architectural progress, we might preserve a quaint, historic Mouraria, alien to the polemic quarter, to the west of Rua da Mouraria: "Lisbon's Mouraria . . . still exists. This 'still' manages to console us, those of us who want a healthy and modern Lisbon, but who are afraid that they will take away whatever remains of that picturesque Mouraria that never hurt a soul."[2]

As Araújo was an *olissipógrafo* [scholar of Lisbon's history] in the pre-Republican tradition of José Pinto de Carvalho, Júlio de Castilho, and Júlio Dantas, he vehemently disdained the sacrifice of Lisbon's material history for the sake of urban rehabilitation. Araújo's *Peregrinações em Lisboa* (1938) and *Legendas de Lisboa* (1943) constitute denunciations of the modernization of Lisbon during the 1930s in their glorification of the capital's architectural treasures. Therefore, Araújo's apology of the CML's destruction of the Baixa Mouraria and its apparently inevitable demolition of the *fadista* quarter seems incongruous to his nostalgic pilgrimage to Rua do Capelão. Despite his defense of the Estado Novo's motivations for the "Salvação Barreto" project, Araújo clamors futilely to save some vestige of the Mouraria by appealing to Lisboners' appreciation of a pre-Republican aristocratic quarter. Thus, he reminds us of the Mouraria's other faces so often obscured by the sordid shadow of the Fado: "The part was taken for the whole and, thus, that [*fadista*] Mouraria became famous: a street, four alleys were understood to be an entire neighborhood."[3]

Nevertheless, the deplorable conditions of the Mouraria's architecture were exaggerated further by the neighborhood's reputation as one of Lisbon's red-light districts. Suzanne Chantal's apocalyptic vision of an eighteenth-century Lisbon in which the streets are littered with excrement and animal carcasses, and José Inácio dos Santos Cruz's depiction of a nineteenth-century Mouraria, rife with venereal diseases, appear to be contemporary accounts in the 1930s and 1940s that reconcile the "Salvação Barreto" program's intention to level the entire Mouraria and rebuild a quarter that might reflect the Estado Novo's goals of economic unity in its construction of sumptuous and modest homes in the same neighborhood.[4]

However, at the turn of the twentieth century, such utopian class unity underpins Dantas's play and novel in which the noble sixteenth- and seventeenth-century Mourarias are little more than a backdrop for the *cafés de lepes* [cheap coffee houses] and brothels of the nineteenth-century Rua do Capelão. In consideration of the limits of the stage and, perhaps, the attention span of the reader of light literature, Dantas confines the Mouraria to the *fadista* quarters of Ruas do Capelão, da Amendoeira, and da Mouraria. Nevertheless, the other, noble Mouraria is present in Dantas's work. The characterization of the Count of Marialva and the Marchioness of Ceide complements that of Severa and Custódia. The props of the noble litters and horse-drawn carriages contrast with the laundry wagon into which Severa escapes the prison of Marialva's palace. The opera at the São Carlos Theatre in the Chiado is a prelude to Severa's Fados in a tavern on Travessa do Poço da Cidade in the Bairro Alto. And we hear the crude slang of the carriage drivers and the gypsy horse grooms alongside the gentility of the aristocrats' refined speech.

Dantas portrays the Mouraria as a privileged, autonomous space in which otherwise incongruous elements of society exist on par. Here, gentlemen regard prostitutes as lovers, and muleteers as confidants. Pacts are made between *fadistas* and noblemen that seem impossible outside of the popular quarter, where the *fadista* is treated as an exotic import from the degraded neighborhoods where the flash of a knife resolves any cultural misunderstandings between the dissimilar social groups.[5]

Although Dantas's Mouraria may seem idealistic in its treatment of the interaction between noblemen and *fadistas*, it is not entirely fictitious. The Mouraria, like Lisbon's other popular riverside neighborhoods and prior to the widening of Rua da Palma in the 1930s, was characterized by social contrasts; here the poor and the noble lived side by side. We might say that Faria da Costa's projected social unity in his urbanization of Alvalade already had taken place willingly in the pre-Republican Mouraria: the Mouraria slated for demolition to build a new utopia characterized by socioeconomic integration; a neighborhood in which a variety of homes, corresponding to a variety of classes, might blend seemlessly.[6]

The *fado novo* of the 1930s to 1970s reproduces the archetypal relationship of the nobleman and the prostitute—exemplified by Severa and the Count of Vimioso/Marialva—in its *fados de contraste* that narrate an impracticable love between the *fadistas* of Ruas do Capelão and da Amendoeira and noble *amadores de fado* [Fado aficionados]. In the outdated Romantic tradition of Dantas's play and novel, these love affairs are rendered impossible by the social disparity of the lovers. Nevertheless, the narration of these relationships in the *fado novo* draws our attention to the privileged social autonomy of the pre-Republican Mouraria, a reality that is echoed in the coexistence of palaces and whorehouses in the same urban quarter. After the Palace of the Marquis of Alegrete is slated for demolition in the 1930s, the *fados de contraste* serve to criticize the Estado Novo's plans for unity among different classes by indicating the irony of its venture: the demolition of a Mouraria where the poor and the aristocrats already converged:

Naquela casinha
Morou a Severa
No tempo passado
E o Alegrete
Fidalgo que era
Vizinho do fado.[7]

[In that little house
Severa lived
In days gone by
And the Marquis of Alegrete
A nobleman who was
The Fado's neighbor.]

By reproducing the Romantic fatality of these nineteenth-century amorous relationships between *fadista* and aristocrat, the *fado novo* denounces the CML's demolition of the Mouraria by way of allegory to the erasing of the architectural testimony of social unity between the poor and the rich. Thus the impossibility of a union between the lower classes and the nobility, because of social prohibitions in a pre-Republican Lisbon, is signaled in the "Salvação Barreto" project's erasing of the vestiges of an architectural union between *fadistas* and aristocrats. By accusing the CML of undemocratic maneuvers in its destruction of the Mouraria, the *fado novo* questions the seemingly democratic justification of the projected demolitions that sought to force cohabitation between the poor and the bourgeoisie.

In 1938, even Norberto de Araújo appears to favor the pending demolition of the ruins of the Palace of the Marquis of Alegrete and its neighboring buildings, an area he calls "ugly, unpleasant, despite its local color."[8] However, five years later, he laments the leveling of the palace's arch as he bemoans the demolition of the Mouraria: "The Arch of the Palace of the Marquis of Alegrete—the old gate of Saint Vincent on the [Fernandine Wall]—passage from the Baixa to the Mouraria in the most picturesque nook of all of Lisbon, against which lean the ruins of the Palace."[9] Could half a decade of the CML's chipping away at the site of one of Araújo's pilgrimages have turned the author against the progress that he had justified as being "obedient to the city's blueprint for urban reform"?[10] Had the Estado Novo's and CML's modernization gone too far? By 1943, Araújo's complaint echoes the complaints of the *fado novo* in its fatalistic vision of the threatened Mouraria: "The quarter drowns in the twists and turns of Rua dos Canos, and the Mouraria continues up to the Poço do Borratém on the same shaky clothesline."[11] The author employs a tone of defeat—in a rhetorical style that mimics the *fado novo*'s impotent nostalgia in the face of progress, to call Lisboners' attention to the erasing of eight centuries of urban history in two decades: "And there you have the Mouraria, once the medieval city of the Moorish commune—an etching that kept fading."[12]

The nostalgia of *fados novos* set in the pre-Republican Mouraria blurs epochs in the Fado's diachronic evolution. Anachronisms and ellipses confuse decades, as musicians of the early twentieth century become contemporaries of *fadistas* of the mid-nineteenth. A vague longing for a lost Mouraria dominates as literary and legendary allusions subordinate historical accuracy. Love affairs between aristocracy and the *fadista* class yield to the pressures of codes that predominate outside the Mouraria. The lovers accept the impossibility of their union in the face of a changing Mouraria, threatened by progress, as the material vestiges of a noble quarter are annulled in Lisbon's modernization. The demolition of the Palace of the Marquis of Alegrete, on the edge of the *fadista* Mouraria, erases the architectural evidence of a socially egalitarian urban quarter as the CML's bulldozers close in on Rua do Capelão. And the *fadista* resigns him- or herself to visiting the ghosts of the alluded Mouraria by consciously reconstructing its nineteenth-century avatars in verse.

The *fado novo* ignores the Mouraria that until the seventeenth century was a suburb, most remembered as home to those marginalized or expelled from inside Lisbon's walls. *Fadistas* focus on the nineteenth century—seemingly the neighborhood's most democratic period—during which Lisbon came to the *Moirama.* In this questionable portrait of conviviality between all strata of urban society, Dantas's figures of the prostitute and the Count become commonplace and no longer signify the contextual circumstances of the relationship between Severa and Vimioso/Marialva. We toss about the generic expressions *severas*, *marialvas*, and *vimiosos*, thus cementing the artificial folklorization of a *fadista* Mouraria derived from a literary referent grounded in historical/biographical testimony. *Novos fadistas* of the twentieth century appropriate the history of the Fado to serve their propagandistic interests; lyricists and *fadistas* reconstruct an idealized Mouraria characterized by cohabitation between aristocrats and prostitutes and, seldom, noblewomen and ruffians: a quarter in which the social hierarchy of a pre-Republican Lisbon does not exist.[13] The threatened Mouraria is observed as a socially autonomous space; for better or worse, its inhabitants are neither subject to social nor legal codes. The lawlessness of Dantas's Rua do Capelão yields to a carnivalesque Largo da Severa in which the caste and the outcast are free from such class distinctions.

In this reconstructed Mouraria, nineteenth-century historical figures recede, as Dantas's literary characters become archetypes of social contrast, recalled in an oneiric mist to remind us of a Lisbon that quickly is disappearing. Already, at the turn of the twentieth century, Pinto de Carvalho recognized a trend that would characterize the *fado novo*'s relationship to his contemporary, Dantas's memory of Severa: "Fleeting romance, sensual frivolity, friendships often subject to caution, all of this leaked love potions into the veins of the ruffians of the era, stirred their minds, and incensed their flesh, in the same way that, years later, it would haunt the Bacchic dreams of the *fadistas*, dreams in which Severa's image would pass by like the phantom of Desire, irritating and fugacious."[14] "Fado Sonho" and "O Fado à Luz da Candeia" exploit the seemingly illogical order of dreams and the hallucinatory effect of light, alluded in their titles, to create an idealized Mouraria: a folkloric pastiche that distorts the quarter's historical character by resetting it in the impressionistic haze of a candle's glow.[15]

In "Fado Sonho," the singer disdains the *fado novo* in his homage to the supposed *fado castiço* of nineteenth-century *fadistas* and aristocrats, incarnate in *severa(s)* and *vimioso(s):*

Era o fado mas o fado rigoroso
Cantava-o a Severa a preceito
Com a guitarra nas mãos do Vimioso
Tangia anseios de fogo no peito.

[It was the Fado, the classical Fado
Severa used to sing it correctly
[And] with a Portuguese guitar in his hands
Vimioso's strumming started a fire in Severa's bosom.]

The twentieth-century *fadista*, compelled by a composite image—part Dantas's literary fancy, part history—of a pre-Republican Mouraria that haunts his subconscious, picks up a Portuguese guitar to sing a *desgarrada* [duet] with Severa: "E eu então fadista como era / Peguei numa guitarra e fui tocar / Cantei ao desafio com a Severa" [So I, being a *fadista* / Picked up a Portuguese guitar and started to play / And I challenged Severa to a duet]. But the twentieth-century *fadista* awakens from his dream to lament that the alluded Mouraria is extinct: "Mas isto meus senhores / Foi a sonhar" [But that, ladies and gentleman / Was just a dream].

In a similar manner, "O Fado à Luz da Candeia" reorganizes memories of various *fadista* Mourarias in which prostitutes, illuminated by the glow of gas lamps, serenaded aristocrats:

Outrora na Mouraria
Que foi seu berço fagueiro
Pra cantar à fidalguia
Queria a luz dum candeeiro.

[Long ago in the Mouraria
The tender birthplace of the Fado
They sang to the noblemen
In the spotlight of a gas lamp.]

In this ahistorical context, Dantas's Severa appears as the archetype of the twentieth-century folkloric vision of the nineteenth-century prostitute:

Dizem que a Severa amada
Quando se punha a cantar
Queria a luz apagada
Pra que não a vissem chorar.

[They say that our beloved Severa
Whenever she started singing
Wanted the lights out
So that nobody could see her crying.]

And the *fadista* Mouraria prior to the widening of Rua da Palma (1931) is mourned whenever Fado is sung by candlelight: a prayer in memory of Severa and her posthumous Armandinho:

Com uma candeia acesa
O fado em qualquer cantinho
É oração que se reza
À Severa e Armandinho.[16]

[With a lit candle
In any corner, the Fado
Is a prayer in honor
Of Severa and Armandinho.]

What was the nature of class mingling between *fadistas* and nobility in the nineteenth-century Mouraria?

After Portugal's Liberal Revolution (1820), Brazil's independence (1822), *Miguelismo* (1828), and the Civil War (1832–34), the *modinha* and the *lundum* disappeared from noble salons because they were considered provincial musical genres associated with the *Antigo Regime* [Old Guard].[17] Italian and French opera supplanted Luso-Brazilian songs as Lisbon's intellectuals and dandies imported cosmopolitan customs and tastes.[18] In Dantas's novel, the Portuguese aristocracy attends the opera at the São Carlos Theater, as if obliged to comply with Lisbon's fashionable internationalization. Yet, the Count of Marialva is seduced by rumors of a talented young *fadista* in the Bairro Alto. When Dantas's character, the Marquis of Nisa, speaks of Severa to his friends, he signals the seemingly irreconcilable predilections of the aristocracy at the time of the Cabrais: "Did you know that, in the Bairro Alto, we have our own little [Virginia] Boccabadati who makes people cry when she sings the Fado? . . . A perfect example of Fado, sung with her heart in her throat, a Fado that is worth all of Italy's Opera."[19] In a similar manner, in Dantas's description of Marialva's wardrobe, he indicates the aristocrat's underlying contradiction in tastes: "Anyone who saw him dressed up in his satin vest and his silver-buttoned jacket, certainly would not recognize him as the close friend of the carriage drivers and horse grooms, the honorary lover of the whores of *Rua Suja*, such was the aristocratic gentility of his demeanor, such was the natural elegance of his gestures, the refined distinction of his French cuffs from which shined two big, bluish gems."[20] Marialva's aesthetic conflict between the high-brow, imported genre and the local plebeian song signals noble nostalgia for lost values; a nostalgia that pervades all classes in a politically unstable Portugal of the 1840s: "a country shaken, even poorer than it had been, devastated by successive wars."[21] Vieira Nery characterizes the Fado's appeal to disparate sectors of urban society as "an implied agreement between two very distinct groups that share a common heritage based on their common memories of the *Antigo Regime.*"[22] The Lisbon Fado manifests a communal longing for an autochthonous, urban musical expression: a cathartic throwback to a Lisbon before the French invasion of 1807.[23]

The solidarity of the various social classes, unified in their disenchantment with the turmoil of recent regimes, yields to a reevaluation of class stratification. However, the *fado novo* exaggerates the promiscuous abandon of social hierarchy in its portrait of a democratic Mouraria in which the *fadista*, the bourgeois and the aristocrat are equals. Miguel Queriol's memory of a subdued Severa, out of place among nobility, at the Count of Vimioso's palace in Campo Grande, indicates the problematic social imbalance resulting from the nobility's and petit-bourgeoisie's forays into the bordellos of the Mouraria, and the consequent debut of the Mouraria *fadista* in noble salons.[24]

The "Fado do Embuçado" paints an optimistic portrait of such *marialva* socialism, by giving the impression of an open-door policy between all classes:

N'outros tempos a fidalguia
Que deu brado nas toiradas
Andava p'la Mouraria
E em certo palácio havia
Descantes e guitarradas.[25]

[Long ago the nobility
Who cut quite a figure in the bullring
Wandered around the Mouraria
And in many palaces
Guitar solos and duets were heard.]

Yet this Fado, like many others, obscures the less Romantic reality that the nobility came to the Mouraria to exploit its prostitutes. The nobility entered the Mouraria willfully, whereas the *fadistas* came to their noble salons exclusively by invitation. By chance, the Count of Vimioso stumbled upon the Mouraria's most talented *fadista.* The resulting cultural exchange—if we can call it such—consisted of showcasing the poor, often criminal singers, in a palatable milieu to justify the nobility's jaunts into the whorehouses of the Mouraria, by disguising the aristocrats' indiscretions as philanthropic patronage of the artists.

The aristocracy who hitherto had disdained the *fadista* class was, for the first time, inviting indigents and prostitutes from the Mouraria into their palaces. After Severa's death in 1846, various sectors of Lisbon's society embrace the novelty of the Fado. Intellectuals, journalists, actors, artists, and the bourgeoning middle class socialize with Mouraria prostitutes/*fadistas* in the 1860s, following the assumed model of daring social unity practiced by bullfighting noblemen such as the Count of Anadia, the Marquis of Belas, and the Marquis of Castelo-Melhor. However, the encounter between the aristocrats and the *fadistas* always amounts to caprice, and inevitably the lovers return to their respective social classes.

The Fado "O Marquês de Linda-a-Velha" recognizes the ephemeral nature of class mixing in the nineteenth-century Mouraria in its narration of a love affair between a noble Fado aficionado and Júlia, an apocryphal *fadista*, from Rua da Amendoeira.[26] The Mouraria *fadista* is the main attraction at the Marquis's Palace where:

Lá dentro há ramboia e farra
E o Marquês toca guitarra
Para a Júlia da Amendoeira
E nos salões do Marquês
Há palmas de quando em vez
Aos motes da cantadeira.

[Inside there is a wild party
And the Marquis plays the Portuguese guitar
For Júlia from Rua da Amendoeira
And in the Marquis's salons
You hear clapping from time to time
For the singer's ballads.]

However, when the Marquis's lover—"Senhora nobre de fama / Nos anais de fidalguia" [A noble lady / Famous in the annals of the aristocracy]—arrives in a carriage, the music stops and everyone looks at her: "Ela entrou calou-se tudo / E nesse ambiente mudo / Uma voz sobressaiu" [She entered and everyone hushed / And in that silent room / A voice stood out]. Júlia sings her Fado and leaves the palace, resigned

Maria Severa's house on Rua do Capelão, photograph by Susana Correia.

that a prostitute from the Mouraria cannot compete with a Marchioness: "A Júlia altiva e bizarra / Cantou mesmo sem guitarra / Um fado triste e saiu" [Júlia, haughty and valiant/ Sang a sad Fado / A cappella, and she left].

The last verse of the Fado, however, reveals the irony of the noble appropriation of the Fado, often glossed over in a fever to restore the Fado's image by attributing it to the good tastes of the rich. We are led to believe that the Marquis truly loved Júlia because now: "O Marquês vive isolado / Pois nunca mais se ouviu o fado / Nos salões de Linda-a-Velha" [The Marquis lives alone / And the Fado was never heard again / In the salons of Linda-a-Velha]. However, this Fado draws our attention to the privileged space of the nineteenth-century Mouraria as a locus of social convergence between disparate classes. Simultaneously it reveals the injustice of Júlia's banishment from the Marquis's Palace: the impossibility of class mingling outside of the Mouraria. And Júlia's return to the Mouraria is a homecoming to the cradle of the Fado: the host of noble/plebeian romances and the site of their demise.

However, the Mouraria is not the only space in which the constraints of class attenuate. By the 1850s, the Fado is recontextualized in conspicuous, socially ambiguous settings: bullrings, *frescatas* [picnics], salons, and theaters, where, despite an inevitable perpetuation of social hierarchy, *fadistas*, the petit-bourgeoisie, and aristocracy are entertained by the same musical spectacle: singing prostitutes and ruffians. But, as Osório indicates, "the Fado evolves and decks itself out in pearls," as a result of its brush with Lisbon's aristocracy.[27] And though the Fado's reputation benefited from the aristocrats' appropriation of the song, the musical genre suffered alterations under the tutelage of a refined public: "[the Fado] abandons its 'popular, spontaneous phase' to begin its 'aristocratic and literary [phase].' "[28] By the time the fictional Júlia da Amendoeira sang at the palace in Linda-a-Velha, the alluded Fado had molded itself to noble tastes.

The Mouraria *fadista*, always a reviled parasite of urban society, occupies center stage in mainstream intellectual life when João Maria dos Anjos and a band of musicians and *fadistas* give a concert at the Casino Lisbonense on May 3, 1873.[29] As a consequence, the Mouraria Fado is distorted by the principles of good taste. Songs are censored of slang and references to violence and sex; and the nineteenth-century Mouraria *fadista*—the ruffian with bell-bottom trousers or the prostitute with a knife hidden in her garter belt—is dressed up for the delicate tastes of the mainstream society, strangled by the alien values and courtesies of the nobility and the middle class.

Nevertheless, the *fadista* complies with the prescribed image. Perhaps Pimentel is correct when he attributes the mid- to late-nineteenth-century aristocratization of the Fado to a vulgar longing for a second coming of a Severa and a young Count.[30] Osório remarks, "in Fado collections we find many allusions to the aristocrats' predilection for the song, which naturally flattered the *fadistas*."[31] The sustained popularity of the cliché trope of the impossible, Romantic love between noblemen and Mouraria prostitutes—apparent in the many recordings of "O Marquês de Linda-a-Velha" and "Novo Fado da Severa (Rua do Capelão)," in the twentieth century—constitutes what Osório calls "folklore's old hack," in which "Prince Charming . . . rescues the stray cat."[32]

In 1874, Júlio César Machado protests the sanitization of the Mouraria Fado for the sterile tastes of the bourgeoisie and nobility:

> The *fadista*, as far as Lisbon understood and worshipped him, was a fierce figure . . . but since the noblemen and the dandies want to become *fadistas*, the *fadistas* too want to become noblemen and dandies, and we cannot count on them anymore; they come out wearing elegant overcoats, with the pomp of virtuosos, to give concerts at the casino and at the circus, and the only thing that we can get them to do for us is sing about the lives of Solomon and David.[33]

Machado's quip is echoed in the lyrics of "Biografia do Fado":

Perguntam-me pelo fado
Eu conheci
Era um ébrio era um vadio
Que andava na Mouraria
Talvez ainda mais magro
Que um cão galgo
E a dizer que era fidalgo
Por andar com a fidalguia.[34]

[You asked me about the Fado
I have met him
He used to be a drunkard and a bum
Who wandered around the Mouraria
He was even skinnier
Than a greyhound

And he told everybody that he was an aristocrat
Just because he went around with noblemen.]

We must recognize the irony of such a fate. The nobility of the 1840s and 1850s sought the Fado in its sordid, native environment of the Mouraria's brothels as an escape from the outdated values of a disenchanted aristocracy whose end was imminent. Nevertheless, the same nobility imposed its aesthetics and ideals on the very *fadista* class that had been its carnivalesque salvation from quotidian decadence.

Let us contrast Queriol's characterization of a demure Severa, suffocated by the foreign tranquility of an evening at Vimioso's palace, to Palmeirim's amusing brush with the *fadista*, at ease in her habitat in the Bairro Alto: "[Severa] spoiled me with a series of insults to which I responded quickly, yielding to her rather unflattering comeback, from which I defended myself and thus impressed her, as she was not expecting to find a fop capable of answering her back at every turn."[35] We are reminded of Severa's historical / literary flight from virtual exile in Vimioso's / Marialva's palace in Campo Grande, to return to the libertine Fado of the whorehouses of the Bairro Alto and the Mouraria, where the song is uncontaminated by the restrictions of bourgeois and noble shame and proliferates as more than a pretext for the aristocracy to visit bordellos. This is the Rua do Capelão where "Severa often treated to wine—a drink that she liked a bit too much—anyone who wanted to drain from his reddish cup the royal blood of the vine"; the Mouraria where Severa "lived among *fadistas* in the confusion of cigarettes and pints [of wine]."[36] When Lisbon's dandies and intellectuals tire of their complicity with the watered-down version of Fado, they too abandon the consecrated venues to return anonymously to the Mouraria, where the song still thrives in a purer, more indecorous form.

Nevertheless, in the *fado novo*'s unfaithful memory of the nineteenth century, the *fado liró* [noble Fado] is idealized. In "Encontro com o Fado," the Fado that results from the mingling of classes—the same Fado that Machado criticizes for adulterating the *fado bairrista* of the popular neighborhoods—inaccurately is characterized by its authenticity:

Fado d'antigamente
Era mais belo
E mais bairrista

Deixava sempre na gente
Um sabor todo fadista.[37]

[Yesterday's Fado
Was more beautiful
And more authentic
It often left us
With a real *fadista* taste in our mouths.]

If anything, nineteenth-century aristocratic patronage of the Fado and the consequent exportation of the song to noble salons were detrimental to neighborhood traditions. The *fado novo*'s proposal of a causal relationship between the nineteenth-century nobility's trend of slumming and *bairrismo* credits the golden age of the Fado to the decay of social hierarchy in the pre-Republican Mouraria, perhaps because: "Em tempo da fidalguia / Lisboa vivia ainda a sonhar" [In the time of the monarchy / Lisbon still had dreams].

Yet, the alluded Mouraria of counts and dandies is responsible for the first stages of decadence in the song's evolution from the crude, primordial *fado batido* to *fado novo*. However, the *fado novo* of the 1930s to 1970s claims the impure, aristocratic Fado as the roots of the national song as a means to reconstruct the reputation of the *fadista*. The *fado novo*'s erroneous understanding of the relationship between *marialvismo* and the diachronic evolution of the Fado as a musical genre is, in part, responsible for promoting the folkloric image of a lost, Romantic Mouraria: "Estava em festa a Mouraria / Quando a Severa lá ia cantar" [The Mouraria was alive / When Severa sang there].

Just as Dantas's theatrical and novelistic recreations of the Mouraria at the time of the Cabrais are set on Ruas do Capelão and da Amendoeira and Largo da Guia, the *fado novo*'s scenes of conviviality between ruffian and aristocrat are set in the *fadista* quarter. Dantas chose his locus as the most relevant context for his dramatization/fictionalization of Severa's biography. However, the lyricists of the *fado novo* of the 1930s to 1970s stake their ground in Dantas's *fadista* Mouraria to reclaim it as the last frontier of tradition in Lisbon's old Moorish Quarter, the only remaining vestige of the supposed origins of the Lisbon Fado. It is the site of the houses where the Count of Vimioso kept Severa—thus the epicenter of *fadista* Lisbon—the remarkable neighborhood where pre-Republican social hierarchies first crumble when the Mouraria hosts nobility, prostitutes, vagrants, and intellectuals under the same roof.

If we believe, as the *fado novo* recommends, that the traditional, homegrown *fado bairrista* was born of the union between aristocrat and prostitute in the Mouraria, then it reasons that the destruction of that Mouraria, in the demolition of architectural vestiges of cohabitation between nobility and prostitutes, should be blamed for the allegorical death of the Fado. As we have observed in the previous chapter, *fados novos* abound in which Severa's death is tantamount to the death of the Fado, Severa's death signals the death of the Mouraria, and the death of the Mouraria is the death of the Fado.

But the Fado is reborn in Maria Severa's 1846 death and rises triumphantly in the ash of the CML's mid-twentieth-century demolition of the Baixa Mouraria. Whereas historical works between the publication of Santos Cruz's *Da Prostituição na Cidade de Lisboa* (1841) and Moita's *O Fado, Canção de Vencidos* (1936) demystify the prostitution of the Mouraria, Dantas's and Leitão de Barros's Romantic treatments of the relationship between the *fadista* and the aristocrat during the first three decades of the twentieth century, set the tone for the *fado novo* of the 1930s to 1970s. And although the Mouraria of *severas* and *marialvas* does not exist by the turn of the twentieth century, the most salient folkloric memories of the quarter are characterized by social unity between noblemen and *fadistas*.

Although the aristocratic appropriation of the Fado has improved the song's reputation and, perhaps, promoted its status as national song in the mid-twentieth century, the Fado's consequent popularity among all strata of Portuguese society has altered the musical genre. Osório believes that the nineteenth-century Fado degraded into *fado novo* because the singers were no longer members of a *fadista* class. As a result, the experience in the Fado house became more staged: "The Fado is mutilated and ceases to express a human condition, a concrete way of life. Its setting becomes more and more artificial, because the human sub-class that once expressed it starts to disappear."[38] In Osório's opinion, tourism deals the Fado its most wounding, but not fatal blow, and thus reduces the song to "a wailing, mawkish postcard . . . a whining chant."[39]

In the touristic memory of a pre-Republican Lisbon, prostitutes, murderers, and thieves of the Mouraria are reset as folkloric types. Their unnamed crimes seem innocuous: a consequence of their marginal inclusion in noble society. The distance of memory distorts the Mouraria's history. As Lisbon's most threatened historic quarter lacks material vestiges of its earlier avatars, the *fado novo* refers to recent memories as the neighborhood assumes the colorful characteristics of Júlio Dantas's and Leitão de Barros's artificial reconstruction of the Mouraria. What remains is the theatrical and cinematic Mouraria.

The Fado, "O Café de Camareiras" signals the theatrical elements inherent in the twentieth-century *fado novo*'s nostalgic interpretation of that nineteenth-century Mouraria of *severas* and *vimiosos*.[40] By drawing our attention to the dramatic character of the *fado novo*'s reconstruction of the nineteenth-century Mouraria, "O Café de Camareiras" underlines the Fado's need to rescue the Mouraria that has disappeared in the Estado Novo's demolition projects.

The opening verse of the Fado announces the Mouraria's condition as mere memory by identifying the *fadista*'s role as narrator for the sake of the neighborhood's posterity:

Vou fazer a descrição
Do café de camareiras
No bairro da Mouraria
Lembrar tempos que lá vão
De fidalgos e rameiras
E cenas de valentia.

[I am going to describe
The *café de camareiras*
In the Mouraria
And recall days gone by
Of aristocrats and whores
And acts of bravery.]

But even within the *(novo) fadista*'s lifetime, the *café de camareiras* had become a dramatic spectacle for Lisboners avid to peer in on the criminal Mouraria:

Os rufias são actores
No teatro da ralé
Por isso ninguém se ilude
Nós somos espectadores
E o teatro é o café
Do cantinho da Saúde.

[The ruffians are actors
In the theater of the scum
No one is fooled

We are mere spectators
And the theater is the coffee shop
On the corner of (the Church of Nossa Senhora da) Saúde.]

The artifice of the theater is revealed as the movements at the cafe are characterized as scenes and acts: "E é bom que ninguém se afoite / Vão-se dar cenas canalhas / Nestes actos de má fé" [Don't ruffle your feathers / You are going to see some tasteless scenes / In these acts of bad faith]. The anti-heroes enter punctually, as if on cue: "Deram dez horas de noite / Entrou a rusga às navalhas / Pelas portas do café" [The clock struck ten / And the thugs entered with their knives drawn / Through the doors of the cafe]. The ruffians, as if in a naturalistic play, speak in slang: "Os rufias falam calão." And the interaction between the ruffian and the prostitute appears to be a choreographed dance:

E uma camareira esperta
Chegou-se com ligeireza
Prà mesa dum rufião
E tirando a navalha aberta
Que ele espetara na mesa.

[And a crafty hooker
Undaunted, approached
The ruffian's table
And she pulled out the knife
That he had stabbed into the tabletop.]

The prostitutes and *fadistas* enter to bring a tone of levity to the scene:

Depois da rusga abalar
Entraram muitas rameiras
E há movimento e alegria
E há fadistas a cantar
Várias cenas desordeiras.

[After the thugs had left
Many whores entered
And there was energy and happiness
And *fadistas* were singing
Chaos ensued.]

Nevertheless, the Fado's bitter last line reminds us that such a Mouraria no longer exists: "Era assim a Mouraria" [That's how the Mouraria used be].

The well-intentioned yet failed "Salvação Barreto" program proposes to bring progress to Lisbon's riverside by building housing projects for a variety of classes. However, to make room for the socially diverse urban development, the CML must demolish neighborhoods—Mouraria and Alfama—inhabited by both the bourgeoisie and the poor. To build the Estado Novo's social utopia, the "Salvação Barreto" program eradicates the Baixa Mouraria, a quarter that in terms of architecture, and in terms of its own social codes, alludes to Lisbon's first breakdown of class stratification.

The lyrics of the *fado novo* idealize a pre-Republican Mouraria in its recreation of Dantas's Rua do Capelão, to denounce the Estado Novo's sacrifice of tradition—the cradle of the Fado—for the sake of its dream of modernization. The *fado novo* exaggerates the camaraderie between the nobility and the *fadistas*, as it recalls social unity in the demolished quarter, by reconstructing Dantas's Mouraria, which is characterized by class mingling, exemplified by the love affair between the Count and Severa. Thus the *fado novo* draws the Estado Novo's and the CML's attention to the counterproductive, and even ironic, nature of their demolition projects.

Furthermore, the Fado purposefully misinterprets its own history by crediting Severa's era in the Mouraria with the golden age of the Fado. While the Fado laments the erasing of its own history in the demolition of noble and *fadista* Mourarias, it simultaneously seizes the opportunity to rewrite its own history in the fictive glow of Dantas's literary fancy. Thus the *fadistas* of the twentieth century attribute the apogee of the Fado with the Mouraria *fadista*'s early and mid-nineteenth-century brush with aristocracy, however, class mingling signals the first stages in the song's decadence as it evolves into *fado novo*. What remains is an artificial folkloric memory of the nineteenth-century Mouraria—borrowed from Dantas's novel and play—and an equally artificial spectacle of Fado performance rooted in the false assumption that the *fado castiço* was born of the union between the aristocracy and the *fadista* classes.

4

The Church of Nossa Senhora da Saúde: The Last Vestiges of a Christian Mouraria and the Gateway to Severa's Rua do Capelão

> I go to the Cathedral, I go up and down Rua da Madalena, I pass by Rua do Poço do Borratém, I go through the Arco do Marquês de Alegrete and I enter the Mouraria. What little remains of that enchanted quarter is nothing compared to its beauty of twenty years ago. The Arch is gone, and there in Largo da Guia, forsaken like a little old lady without a family, is the lovely little Church of Nossa Senhora da Saúde! It is the only thing that remains of all that there once was on the western side of the Mouraria . . . The rest has been demolished. I do not know who was responsible for this crime that destroyed one of my favorite corners [of Lisbon], but I leave him with my curse: May he live to be ninety years old in his nephew's house.
>
> —Beatriz Costa

MARIA SEVERA HARDLY APPEARS IN THE FIRST ONE HUNDRED PAGES of Júlio Dantas's novel because she is attending boarding school, a favor arranged by her mother's (Cesária/Barbuda) paramour, a canon at the Coleginho. Cesária hopes to elude Severa's fate of prostitution by giving her a religious education. However, when the magnanimous cleric dies, Severa must return to her mother's home on Rua do Capelão, where, corrupted by the brothels and the Fado of the popular Mouraria, she becomes the folkloric Severa. Nevertheless, before the reader encounters Dantas's novelistic avatar, he/she confronts an innocent, eight-year-old Severa who escapes her mother's misfortune in the *fadista* quarter, in the sanctuary of a forgiving, Christian Mouraria.

Dantas's Christian Mouraria complements the aristocratic and *fadista* Mourarias in the *fado novo*'s reconstruction of the neighborhood's folkloric identity in its presentation of a Mouraria of contrasts: at once sinful, noble, and pious. The *fado novo* remembers a nineteenth-century district in which palaces share streets with churches, convents, and brothels. The singular setting that serves Dantas's image of the fallen woman who, beneath her mask of sin, is virtuous—a pathetic victim coaxed into a sordid life in the popular neighborhood—has become a cliché in the *fados novos* set in the Mouraria. In "Maria Severa," the *fadista*'s redemption is confirmed when she goes to heaven:

Bem longe onde o luar
O azul tem mais luz
Eu vejo-a a rezar
Aos pés duma cruz.[1]

[Far away where the blue glow
Of the moonlight is brighter
I see her praying
At the foot of a cross.]

In "Quando a Severa Morreu," when the *fadista* dies:

Tangeram sinos
Na Capelinha da Guia
E dois anjos pequeninos
Desceram à Mouraria.[2]

[Bells rang
In the tiny Chapel of Guia
And two little angels
Came down to the Mouraria.]

In "Maria da Cruz," a naïve village woman is deceived by her lover, and becomes a *fadista* in the Mouraria.[3] In a similar manner, the *fado mouraria*, "Malmequer Pequenino," speaks of a woman who sinned and "por amor se fez fadista" [became a *fadista* because of love].[4] Yet the Fado bears the blame for her vice: "Tão longe o fado a levou / Que Deus a perdeu de vista" [The Fado had carried her so far away / That even God lost sight of her]. And in "Na Capelinha da Guia," a woman prays in the Mouraria Chapel to the image of the Virgin Mary, who inspires her to become a *fadista*.[5]

In the *fado novo*, the Mouraria is characterized by its moral ambivalence. Following Dantas's lead, the song shuns Manichaean dichotomies of virtue and vice, and presents the ruffian with a deep-rooted sense of honor—like Custódia who defends Severa—the nobleman whose honor decays in the marginalized neighborhood—like the Count of Marialva who flashes a knife at Custódia—and the prostitute worthy of honor and redemption, exemplified by the moral of César das Neves's "Fado Choradinho":

Das filhas da desventura
Devemos ter compaixão
São mulheres como as mais
Filhas de Eva e de Adão.[6]

[We should be compassionate
Toward the daughters of misfortune
They are women, like any other,
The daughters of Eve and Adam.]

Norberto de Araújo signals Rua do Capelão's complex character in his portrait of the Mouraria's inhabitants: "No other neighborhood has seen such mouths singing and praying, such arms fighting and working."[7] In the *fado novo,* Dantas's and Leitão de Barros's Rua do Capelão assumes a new face as the nexus of the *fadista* quarter that in its memories of processions of a devoutly Christian Mouraria is redeemed in the national folklore:

Eu não consinto que exista
Quem ponha mais devoção
Mais alma, mais coração
Ao cantar a Mouraria.[8]

[As far as I'm concerned there isn't
Anyone who shows more devotion
More soul, more heart
Than the Mouraria when she sings.]

But today's Mouraria is Christian primarily in memory and toponyms, for almost all vestiges of the district's religious past have been erased in the name of progress: the progress of many regimes, even before the Estado Novo. Araújo says of the Mouraria of the late 1930s: "In spite of the modern, and even Modernist buildings that we are going to see, we can still evoke the curfew bell, the nightly passage of the hooded beggars—terror of the children—who ask for wax from Our Lady of the Afflicted, the chanting of songs, the hustle and bustle of the people on their way home from work."[9] The approximate area of the present Mouraria was home to the Mozarabs during the Moorish occupation of Lisbon (714–1147); the Portuguese and Anglo-Norman Pilgrims of the Second Crusade razed that *Moçarabia.*[10] In 1170, St. Vincent of Zaragoza's relics were discovered in the Tagus estuary at the site of Rua do Arco do Marquês de Alegrete, the Portas de São Vicente da Mouraria on the Fernandine Wall (demolished in 1961). In 1258, the Church of São Lourenço was constructed on the ruins of the Mozarab Church of Santa Maria de Alcamim (Santa Justa e Rufina). It was restored in 1867 and rebuilt and incorporated into the Church of São Cristóvão in 1904. In 1273, Dom Afonso III's wife, Queen Dona Brites, established the Colégio dos Meninos Órfãos, later called the Colégio do Menino Jesus; the Coleginho was a police headquarters between 1910 and 1938. The Rosa Convent (1519) had sustained damage in a sixteenth-century tremor and crumbled in 1755, leaving only its annexed Santa Rosa Convent, which disappeared in 1824. The Hermitage of Guia (1600) was the first victim of city planning on Rua da Palma, when the city demolished the small church to open Rua Nova da Palma in 1859. Even the Virgin Mary of Guia had left the Mouraria to stay at the Church of Madalena (near Alfama). She returned to the Mouraria's parish seat, where the 1956 demolitions of the Church of Socorro (1646) compelled the statue's transfer to the Coleginho.

The Christian Mouraria has blocked traffic for centuries: the traffic of the Crusaders' onslaught; the traffic of an early, modern urban society in communication with its nearby produce fields; and, most recently, the traffic between the Baixa and Lisbon's newly incorporated suburbs that would house its growing population. As Lisbon expanded above ground—and underground through its metro system—it became evident that the Mouraria was an obstacle, impeding the wave of progress that would overtake Avenida do Almirante Reis. A visit to today's Mouraria reveals the Estado Novo's extirpation of everything that stood in the way of progress, as modernity ends at the door of the Church of Nossa Senhora da Saúde.

Perhaps by virtue of having survived centuries of destruction in the name of war, earthquakes, urban development, and the Estado Novo's progress, the Church of Nossa Senhora da Saúde is the most relevant architectural remnant of a Christian Mouraria for the *fado novo.* The small church and its four-century-old procession serve as leitmotifs in the *fado novo* of the 1940s to 1960s, as symbols of resistance to the Estado Novo's modernization of Lisbon, while the "Salvação Barreto" urban rehabilitation project threatens to erase the Mouraria. The lyrics of the *fado novo* denounce the Estado Novo's concept of progress by evoking nostalgia for a pre-Republican Mouraria embodied in the Church. In the *fado novo*, the Church of Nossa Senhora da Saúde is a material reminder of both the Christian Mouraria that was demolished in the "Salvação Barreto" project and the pre-Republican architecture that must be saved in the *fadista* quarter to the other side of Rua da Mouraria.

Rua do Capelão's Gabriel de Oliveira wrote "Há Festa na Mouraria" in the 1930s, during the first stages of the Mouraria's rehabilitation.[11] His Fado recalls the extinct Procession of Nossa Senhora da Saúde, interrupted by the First Republic. However, when *fadistas* performed and recorded the song after the procession had reappeared in the Mouraria in 1940, it was set in the memories of a Mouraria that already had vanished: Severa's decadent Mouraria, characterized by prostitution and violent crime.

Gabriel de Oliveira's motifs of the Church of Nossa Senhora da Saúde and its annual procession in "Há Festa na Mouraria" have been appropriated by later Fado lyricists to denounce the "Salvação Barreto" urban rehabilitation project. The evolution of the leitmotifs of the Church, the procession, and the historical and poetic avatars of the song's protagonist, Rosa Maria, in later *fados novos*, confirms that Oliveira's "Há Festa na Mouraria" has inspired a subversive trend in the *fado novo:* the idealization of a pre-Republican Mouraria—emblematized by the Mouraria Church and its procession—as an alternative to the Estado Novo's notion of progress.

Oliveira's Fado tells the story of Rosa Maria, a prostitute on Rua do Capelão who experiences a religious epiphany during the already defunct April 20th procession of Nossa Senhora da Saúde:

Há festa na Mouraria
É dia da procissão
Da Senhora da Saúde
Até a Rosa Maria
Da Rua do Capelão
Parece que tem virtude.[12]

[There is a festival in the Mouraria
It is the day of the Procession of Nossa Senhora da Saúde
Even Rosa Maria
From Rua do Capelão
Seems virtuous.]

Who was Rosa Maria?

Sucena identifies her as "another sad tenant of Rua do Capelão," Oliveira's neighbor, who lived between 1903 and 1945.[13] In the nineteenth century, however, there existed two Rosa Marias in and near the Mouraria who may have inspired Oliveira's character. Pimentel and Sucena write about a Rosa Maria whose Fado house was one of the most celebrated in Alfama at the turn of the twentieth century.[14] And Pinto de Carvalho informs us of a Rosa Maria who lived on Rua do Capelão in the 1830s, who frequented the brothel A Tasca da Rita on Rua da Amendoeira: "She had a lover, a foot soldier, who hid in an alcove of the sordid whorehouse [from which] he attacked and robbed the punters who dared to enter."[15] However, even within Oliveira's lifetime, Rosa Maria reappears in the *fado novo* as the incarnation of the nineteenth-century Mouraria prostitute: a composite of Severa, Scarnicchia, and Maria Petiza.[16] Oliveira's theme of the reverent Mouraria prostitute reverberates in António Amargo's lyrics:

A chorar de arrependida
A cantar com devoção
Uma voz fadista e rude
Aquela Rosa perdida
Da Rua do Capelão
Parece que tem virtude.[17]

[Repentant, crying
Singing with devotion
A gruff *fadista* voice
That wayward rose
From Rua do Capelão
Seems virtuous.]

Aníbal Nazaré and Nelson de Barros's appropriation of the character in "Fado Falado," from the 1947 cabaret show *'Tá Bem ou Não 'Tá*, is evidence of Oliveira's influence on the *fado novo* and demonstrates the Lisbon audience's recognition of his quasi-historical character, even before 1950:

Uma história bem singela
Bairro antigo, uma viela
Um marinheiro gingão
E a Emília Cigarreira
Que ainda tinha mais virtude
Que a própria Rosa Maria
No dia da Procissão
Da Senhora da Saúde.[18]

[A rather unique story
An old quarter, an alley
A swaggering sailor
And Emília Cigarreira
Who was even more virtuous
Than the very Rosa Maria
On the day of the Procession
Of Nossa Senhora da Saúde.]

As a result of the reappearance of the character in popular music, the biographical coincidence with Oliveira's neighbor fades as Rosa Maria is caricatured as a woman of questionable virtue and exploited as a relic of the pre-Republican Mouraria. Zé Manel marries Rosa Maria in the Church of Nossa Senhora da Saúde in the ballad, "O Zé Manel Viu a Rosa Maria."[19] In "O Leilão da Casa da Mariquinhas," the singer meets an older Rosa Maria, "ainda fresca e com gajé" [still fresh and full of life] in the Mouraria.[20] Rosa Maria lends Mariquinhas money to buy back her Portuguese guitar from a pawnbroker when the prostitute is released from prison in "Já Sabem da Mariquinhas."[21] In "Chico Faia," Chiquinho Faia:

Tem sempre ao seu lado
Uma garota prà farra
Chama-se Rosa Maria
Que é para cantar o fado
Enquanto toca a guitarra.[22]

[Always has by his side
A girl for a good time
Her name is Rosa Maria
And she is there to sing Fado
While he plays the Portuguese guitar.]

And "Fui ao Baile" tells the story of a *fadista*'s jealousy when her lover deceives her with Rosa Maria: "Bem vi que falaste com a Rosa Maria /

A tal que tu namoraste / Da Rua da Mouraria" [I saw that you were talking to Rosa Maria / The one whom you used to date / From Rua da Mouraria].[23]

The allusion to Oliveira's Rua do Capelão signals more than autobiographical nostalgia in "Há Festa na Mouraria." Oliveira's Rosa Maria's association with Dantas's mythic/poetic Rua do Capelão identifies her as a prostitute. We recall Rua do Capelão just after the 1755 earthquake where "the women who sold their charms in their windows made explicit gestures."[24] We remember a Mouraria before the Napoleonic invasions that was "a spot on the maps of amorous geography by 1755, and that enjoyed a chilling reputation in eras much earlier than Severa's"; or the *Rua Suja* of the nineteenth century, "visited frequently by English and Portuguese sailors."[25] Nevertheless, the Lisbon audience suppresses the reality of the nineteenth-century Mouraria that Sousa e Costa called "one of the painful cancers of our beautiful capital"; where, "brawls with knives and clubs occurred regularly—all in the name of love—between sailors, soldiers and civilians."[26] We associate Oliveira's Rua do Capelão with the contemporary Rua do Capelão of Leitão de Barros's filmic adaptation of Júlio Dantas's work: the legendary "Dirty Street," "with its sad air of a flesh market" that went to bed at dawn like "a big lesion ashamed of the sun."[27] Dantas's Capelão—an early twentieth-century reconstruction—remains in Lisbon's collective memory, even though the hectic, disorderly Mouraria had already disappeared by the 1880s.[28]

In Oliveira's Fado, as in Dantas's novel and drama, and Leitão de Barros's film, Rua do Capelão's inhabitants are observed with pity: "Those poor, mistreated, sacrificed creatures, subject to all abjection, all misery during a few hours at the flesh market."[29] They are victims of a cruel fate.[30] Here, the *fadistas*, prostitutes, and ruffians are not the scum of Lisbon society of whom Eça de Queiroz, Arroio, and Moita speak in their invectives against the Fado; rather, they appear in the *fado novo* as poor souls who are worthy of charity, regardless of the sordid nature of their lives.

Despite her association with the knife-wielding ruffian, the Mouraria prostitute benefits from popular compassion due to her predisposition for redemption. Sucena indicates the archetype of the reverent prostitute in the Mouraria: "The continuation of the old *Rua Suja* managed to preserve, up until our time, its tradition as a refuge for women of a double fate."[31] Chantal sketches the Mouraria prostitute's daily routine: "Before going out, she blessed herself in front of a small sanctuary, and then she turned up the flame of her lamp three times."[32] Santos Cruz believes that the Lisbon prostitute differs from the Londoner or the Parisian in her religious fervor: "They know perfectly well that there are holy days, in which they must attend mass, they know very well when they must confess, and receive communion; [and] that they should pray; that they should respect and venerate public acts of Religion."[33] Pinto de Carvalho remarks on the Mouraria prostitute, "during lent . . . they all wore hooded capes. Those who did not have one, rented one with pocket change."[34] Palmeirim comments on a religious etching in Severa's apartment in the Bairro Alto.[35] And even in Adelaide da Facada's bedroom, in José Malhoa's painting *O Fado* (1910), we spy images of the crucifixion and Christ's bearing his cross on the way to Golgotha.

Vieira Nery characterizes the treatment of the Mouraria prostitute in nineteenth- and twentieth-century Fados as "a composite sketch of the phenomenon of prostitution, seen from within its emergent social context, and denoting, both a posture of social condemnation and humanitarian compassion."[36] He attributes the trend of moral ambivalence to the legend of Severa: "The unlucky lover of the Count of Vimioso seems to have inspired, from an early age, a vast poetico-musical production, more specifically, in a phenomenon in which diverse [moral] causes are combined."[37] Sousa e Costa believes that Severa was not very religious, if at all, and that she never asked for the sacraments or extreme unction on her deathbed.[38] Nevertheless, we observe a Severa who insisted on being buried in a common unmarked grave with her small varnished crucifix that she wore on her neck, the same neck "where the arms of so many men, thirsty for her kisses, have embraced her."[39]

The narrow Rua da Mouraria separates the Church of Nossa Senhora da Saúde from the site of the famed brothels and Fado houses of the mid-nineteenth century. The proximity of Rua do Capelão to the Church serves Oliveira as a point of contrast between the profane and the sacred to underscore Rosa Maria's moment of redemption during the procession:

Após um curto rumor
Profundo silêncio pesa
Sobre o Largo da Guia
Passa a Virgem no andor
Tudo se ajoelha e reza
Até a Rosa Maria.

[After a brief murmur
Profound silence weighs
Over Largo da Guia
The Virgin passes by in her litter
Everyone kneels and prays
Even Rosa Maria.]

The movement of the procession overwhelms the *fadista* Mouraria, infecting even its most sordid corners with piety. We observe Oliveira's memory of a somber procession:

Naquele bairro fadista
Calaram-se as guitarradas
Não se canta nesse dia
Velha tradição bairrista
Vibram no ar badaladas
Há festa na Mouraria.

[In that *fadista* quarter
The guitars hushed
No one sings on this day
An old local tradition
Bells vibrate in the air
There is a festival in the Mouraria.]

Let us compare António Amargo's recollection of the revered procession:

Tudo aquilo que se preza
De fumar, falar calão
Pôr em praça a juventude
Nessa manhã chora e reza
É dia da Procissão
Da Senhora da Saúde.

[Everything that is cherished
Smoking, speaking in slang,
Youngsters' gathering in the square
[But] on that morning everyone cries and prays
It is the day of the Procession
Of Nossa Senhora da Saúde.]

Araújo, however, remembers a brassier spectacle: "Religious music, military marching bands, local philharmonics; firecrackers, bells, typical noises; 'little angels,' soldiers' wearing red capes on top of their uniforms, and in the [procession's] last thirty years, Prince D. Afonso stands out among the crowds, magnanimous toward his people. Ruas do Capelão, da Amendoeira, do Outeiro, do Coleginho [and] dos Álamos overflowed the Mouraria."[40] Araújo's description corresponds to the procession of 1800–1910. Oliveira's and Amargo's portraits are based loosely on the sixteenth-century procession, first petitioned as an invocation of Saint Sebastian to end the plague.[41]

Oliveira's naïve depiction of a village procession betokens the Mouraria before the First Republic. It remands us to the royal origins of the Church of Nossa Senhora da Saúde, commissioned by D. Sebastião (1569), its procession (1570), and the cessation of the procession, corresponding to the First Republic of 1910.[42] As the "Salvação Barreto" project despoils the Baixa Mouraria of its royal patrimony, the Church of Nossa Senhora da Saúde stands alone as the only relic of a pre-Republican architectural past in the apocalyptic landscape.

The incongruity of the whitewashed village chapel with a Baroque portal, hanging on the edge between the endangered *fadista* Mouraria and the ash and dust of the Estado Novo's progress renders the Church an emblem of the pre-Republican Mouraria, resistant to progress.[43] Its mere presence in the transformed Mouraria defies modernization. The survival of the humble chapel in the context of the Estado Novo's vision of a late twentieth-century Lisbon manifests the people's will to conserve their architectural past by not yielding to the fascistic aesthetics of the neo-Manueline / late Gothic Church of Santo Condestável (1946–51) in Campo de Ourique or the Modernist Church of São João de Brito (1955) in Alvalade.[44]

When Oliveira wrote "Há Festa na Mouraria" in the 1930s, his nostalgia for the pre-Republican procession and his glorification of the nineteenth-century *fadista* quarter did not constitute a criticism of the Republic, it simply complied with the Fado's will to idealize the past. But "Há Festa na Mouraria" transcended its period and became a familiar Fado to later generations because Amália Rodrigues recorded it in 1953, 1967, and 1973.[45] As a result, Oliveira's motif of the Church of Nossa Senhora da Saúde remains in Portuguese popular culture and the mention of the Mouraria Church conjures up memories of "Há Festa na Mouraria." But the symbolic relevance of the motif of the Church assumes new form as the Estado Novo's wrecking ball quickly transforms the lower Mouraria. The Church that in Oliveira's time blended harmoniously with its sixteenth- through nineteenth-century

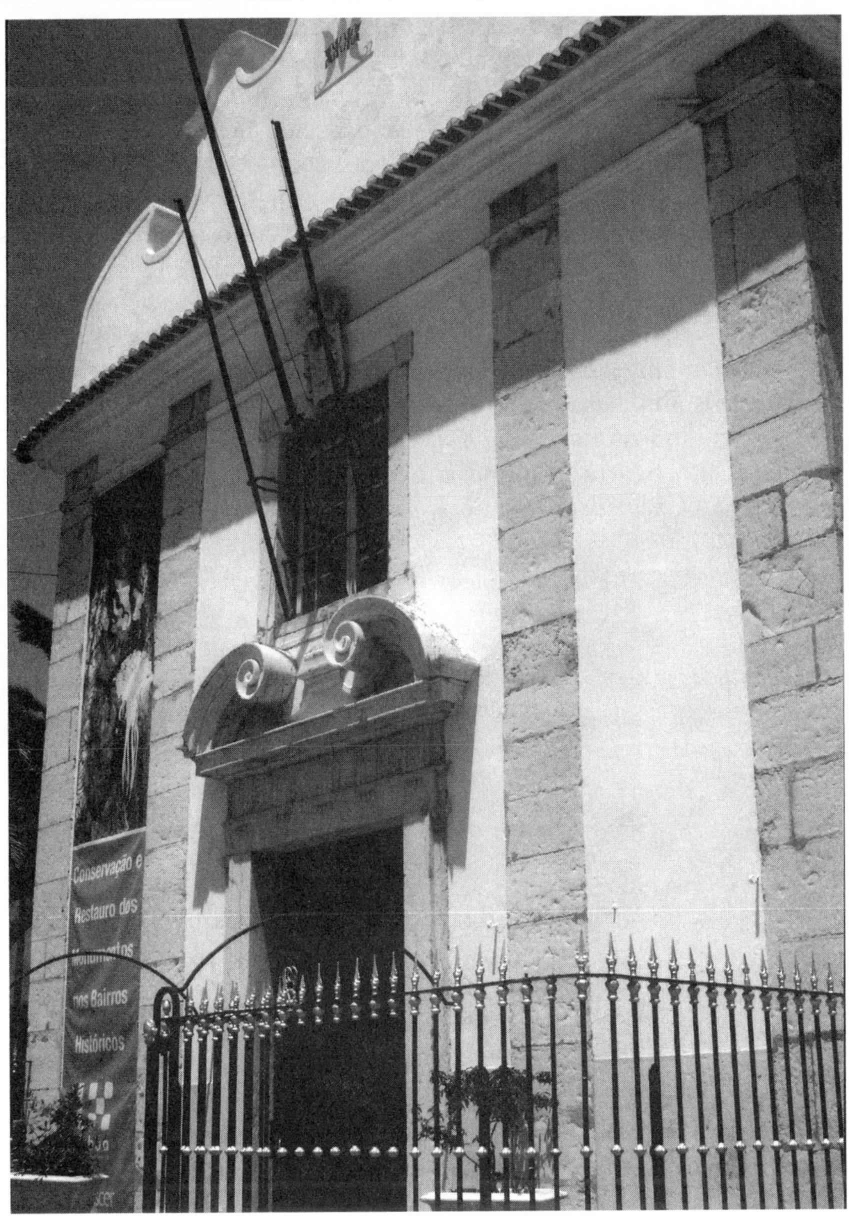

Church of Nossa Senhora da Saúde, photograph by Susana Correia.

surroundings, of a sudden, marked the frontier between a failed rehabilitation project and a threatened patrimony.

The familiar motif of the Church of Nossa Senhora da Saúde is appropriated by Fado lyricists to raise consciousness about the Baixa Mouraria's architectural sacrifice in the name of the Estado Novo's progress. Most Fados appeal to the twentieth-century popularity of the Fado and exploit the consequent historical curiosity about Severa's Mouraria. Thus the Church is seen as a pilgrimage site for the *fadista*, and the Virgem da Saúde [Virgin of Health] serves as a spiritual medium allowing communication between the nineteenth- and twentieth-century singers. The denunciation of the demolition of the Mouraria is implicit in this spiritual encounter.

In "Evocando o Passado," two lovers make a nostalgic pilgrimage to the shell of Severa's Mouraria: Largo da Guia, Rua da Amendoeira, and Rua do Capelão:

Depois juntos os dois
À luz da branca lua
Um rosário de penas
Iremos desfiar
Cantando um fado triste
Ali em qualquer rua
Daquelas onde agora
A dor anda a cantar.[46]

[Later, together
In the light of the white moon
We'll count the beads
On a rosary
Singing a sad Fado
On any of those streets
Where pain sings its song.]

They arrive at the Church of Nossa Senhora da Saúde, where they mourn the destruction of the Mouraria:

E antes que nasça o sol
Em romagem singela
De viela em viela
Em doce melodia

Iremos pra soar
Até junto à capela
Cantares cheios de saudade
O fim da Mouraria.

[And before the sun rises
In a special pilgrimage
From alley to alley
In a sweet melody
All the way up to the Chapel
We'll belt out
Songs full of nostalgia
[And mourn] the death of the Mouraria.]

In "Senhora da Saúde" a *fadista* visits Alfama, Alcântara, Belém, Graça, and the Mouraria to discover the source of her musical inspiration.[47] At four o'clock in the morning, she finds herself at the Mouraria Church where the Virgem da Saúde listens to her Fado:

Às quatro da manhã
Eu reparei que estava
Junta duma capela
Ali na Mouraria
Senhora da Saúde
A santinha benquista
Parece que escutou
As trovas que eu cantei
Senti-me mais mulher
Senti-me mais fadista
Na velha Mouraria
Onde o fado é lei.

[At four o'clock in the morning
I noticed that I was
Standing next to a chapel
In the Mouraria
Senhora da Saúde
The beloved little saint
Seemed to be listening
To the songs that I was singing
I felt like more of a woman
I felt like more of a *fadista*

In the old Mouraria
Where Fado is the law.]

By insisting on the relationship between the Mouraria and the Fado, the lyrics of "Evocando o Passado" and "Senhora da Saúde" remind the Estado Novo of the inherent contradictions of its enterprise. The motif of the Church of Nossa Senhora da Saúde thus serves to admonish the regime against further destroying the Fado's patrimony.

In "Ronda da Saudade," a *fadista* visits four neighborhoods "onde a saudade já mora desde criança" [where nostalgia has always lived]: Madragoa, the Bairro Alto, Alfama, and the Mouraria.[48] In the latter, the personified Rua do Capelão prays to the Virgem da Saúde for Maria Severa's soul—the soul of the Fado and tradition in the Mouraria:

Mouraria faz-me lembrar
Fado, ciúme e virtude
Que um poeta enalteceu
E o Capelão a chorar
Roga à Virgem da Saúde
Pela Severa que morreu.

[Mouraria reminds me
Of Fado, jealousy and virtue
That a poet once venerated
And Rua do Capelão cries and
Prays to the Virgem da Saúde
For Severa's soul.]

I have indicated the Fado's tendency to allude to Severa's death as allegory for the death of the Fado in the destruction of the Mouraria. Such an interpretation takes the Mouraria's salvation out of the Estado Novo's hands and places it in the Virgin's. The lyrics of "Ronda da Saudade" seek the Virgin's intervention against a destructive regime. As a result, this Fado, like "Evocando o Passado" and "Senhora da Saúde," not only pits the regime's notion of progress against a historical conscience, but also, in shrouded terms, against a moral conscience.

Three Fados, popular in the late 1960s and early 1970s, denounce the Estado Novo's well-intentioned progress by idealizing the pre-Republican Mouraria and signaling the Church of Nossa Senhora da

Saúde as an emblem of the golden age of the Fado. I frame the songs "Antigamente," "Fado Pechincha," and "O que Sobrou da Mouraria" within their references to Oliveira's "Há Festa na Mouraria" because of their exploitation of the leitmotif of the Church of Nossa Senhora da Saúde to signal, once again, what went wrong with the "Salvação Barreto" project.[49] I have already mentioned the relevance of Oliveira's Fado in the late 1960s because of Amália Rodrigues's rerecording of it in 1967. The appearance of the leitmotif of the Church of Nossa Senhora da Saúde and its procession in Fados of this period remits us to Oliveira's Fado, which was present in the Portuguese collective conscience. By 1968, however, the leitmotif is heard in tones of regret rather than of the criticism that marked the earlier Fados.

In the dawn of the *primavera marcellista*, censorship waned and the Portuguese explored implicit criticism of the Estado Novo's and Salazar's ideals. In the chief's absence, the country seized the opportunity to forge a regime change in its revolutionary process. The Fado's apparent association with the aesthetic values of the Estado Novo would prove to be its undoing. At a time when the Fado was freer to voice its criticism of the Estado Novo, it seemed to perpetuate the regime's will.[50] However, within the context of the Fado's criticism of the Estado Novo's notion of progress, we may view "Antigamente," "Fado Pechincha," and "O que Sobrou da Mouraria" as the Fado's critical epitaphs; they represent the Fado's last jab at the "Salvação Barreto" project. They propose irrelevant nostalgic values at a moment when Portugal finally conceives of its future. And they signal the closing of a period when anything pre-Republican seemed a viable option for the nation, and the opening of a period coinciding with the dissolution of Portugal's empire.

"Antigamente," like the other Fados that denounce the "Salvação Barreto" project, romanticizes the Mouraria's infamous past of brothels and Fado:

> Antigamente
> Era coito a Mouraria
> Daquela gente
> Condenada à revelia
> E o fado ameno
> Canção das mais portuguesas
> Era o veneno
> Pra lhes matar as tristezas.

[Long ago
The Mouraria was the refuge
Of people condemned to revelry
And the pleasant Fado
The most Portuguese of songs
Was the venom
That killed their sadness.]

"Antigamente" recognizes the lower Mouraria's identity as *o buraco* by defining the district by its void; the Mouraria is identified by what it has lost in the "Salvação Barreto" project:

Nada mais resta
Da moirama que deu brado
Do que a funesta
Lembrança do seu passado.

[Nothing else is left
Of the Moorish quarter that was all the rage
Except for the macabre
Memory of its past.]

And, once again, the song signals irony in the goals of the "Salvação Barreto" project. In the regime's obsession to clean up the Mouraria and extirpate its sordid past, it has made the district even more *fadista:*

Perdeu agora
Todo aspecto de galdéria
Está mais limpa
Está mais séria
Mais fadista cem por cento.

[Now it has lost
Its whorish charms
It is cleaner
More serious
More *fadista* one hundred percent.]

"Antigamente"'s refrain alludes to the context of Rosa Maria's epiphany during the Procession of Nossa Senhora da Saúde in Oliveira's Fado:

A Mouraria
Que perdeu em tempos idos
A nobreza dos sentidos
E o poder duma virtude.

[The Mouraria
That lost in days gone by
The nobility of sensuality
And the power of virtue.]

And we are reminded of "Há Festa na Mouraria" in the Fado's final lines that express a desperate hope for a Mouraria marked by its losses:

Conserva ainda
Toda a graça que ela tinha
Agarrada à Capelinha
Da Senhora da Saúde.

[It still maintains
All of the grace that it once had
Hanging on to the little Chapel
Of Nossa Senhora da Saúde.]

The Mouraria to the east of Nossa Senhora da Saúde is depicted as clinging on to the Church as everything to the west has been turned to rubble.

In a similar manner, "Fado Pechincha" addresses the destruction of the Mouraria with a tone of pessimism and defeat in its first verse:

Fui reviver o passado
Nas ruas da Mouraria
Não vi fadistas nem fado
Desde a Graça até à Guia.

[I went to relive the past
On the streets of the Mouraria
I didn't see *fadistas* or Fado
From Graça down to Rua da Guia.]

Memories of Dantas's Severa are confused with memories of Oliveira's Rosa Maria as the *fadista* visits Ruas da Mouraria and do Capelão:

Um caserio se aninha
Cheio de fé e virtude
Envolto à Capelinha
Da Senhora da Saúde.

[There nests a little house
Full of faith and virtue
Surrounded by the Chapel
Of Nossa Senhora da Saúde.]

Here Severa, like Rosa Maria, is identified by her other faithful, virtuous side: a sketch of the Mouraria of contrasts between the *fadista* and the Christian quarters. Nevertheless, Severa's Fado, as we have mentioned, dies with her:

Foi ali que a Severa
Cantou um fado
E viveu
Mas o fado dessa era
Morreu quando ela morreu.

[That's where Severa
Sang a Fado
And lived
But the Fado of that era
Died when she died.]

While "Antigamente" portrays a *fadista* quarter that has a chance to preserve its tradition by hanging on to its pre-Republican architecture, "Fado Pechincha" has lost hope that what little evidence remains of Severa's Mouraria will be enough to revive tradition in the Mouraria:

E da velha tradição
Já pouco resta hoje em dia
Esses tempos que lá vão
Não voltam à Mouraria.

[And of the old tradition
Very little remains today
Those days that have gone by
Will never return to the Mouraria.]

The *fado canção* "O que Sobrou da Mouraria," from the 1968 musical review *Arroz de Miúdas*, also frames its criticism of the demolition of the Baixa Mouraria within its references to Oliveira's "Há Festa na Mouraria." Unlike "Antigamente" and "Fado Pechincha," "O que Sobrou da Mouraria" sketches a Mouraria identified by its resistance to the "Salvação Barreto" project. The opening verse appropriates the Estado Novo's euphemism of progress to underline the term's irony in such a destructive venture: "Eu nasci na Mouraria / Num prédio que resistia / Ao progresso que venceu" [I was born in the Mouraria / In a building that resisted / The conquest of progress]. Decaying tradition—incarnate in the pre-Republican houses of the Mouraria—is glorified for its rejection of the modern invader. The failed progress is shrugged off as the singer narrates memories of the *fadista* Mouraria, vivid to his contemporaries thanks to Dantas, Leitão de Barros, and the *fado novo*. He makes passing references to the "Novo Fado da Severa": "E toda a gente dizia / Que as ruas da Mouraria / Cheiravam a rosmaninho" [And everybody said / That the streets of the Mouraria / Smelled like rosemary], and to "A Casa da Mariquinhas": "Eram ruas estreitinhas / Janelas com tabuínhas" [There were narrow little streets / Windows with shutters].[51] He creates a pastiche of the mid-seventeenth- and mid-nineteenth-century Mourarias, and reconstructs a Mouraria that had disappeared by 1956, to remind the audience, one last time, of the district that was leveled by the Estado Novo's progress: "E a tal Rua dos Canos / Era a rua dos enganos / Morava ali o pecado" [And Rua dos Canos / Was the street of deception / Sin used to live there].[52] The song, however, demonstrates that the Estado Novo's progress does not penetrate one corner of the Mouraria: "Pequeno prédio gingão / Donde eu via a procissão / Espalhar fé pelo caminho" [A feisty little building / From which I used to watch the Procession / Spreading faith on the street] and that one of the Mouraria's oldest residents will not yield to the regime's modernization:

Mas em cada esquina
Um resto de outrora
A vida deixou
Ai! E na capelinha
Mora uma Senhora
Que não se mudou.

[But on every corner
There is a little bit of yesterday
That life has left behind
Oh! And in the little church
Lives a Lady
Who has not changed.]

"O que Sobrou da Mouraria" takes pride in the defiant figure of the Church of Nossa Senhora da Saúde, and thus epitomizes the *fado novo*'s appropriation of Gabriel de Oliveira's motif in "Há Festa na Mouraria" as the embodiment of the Mouraria that the Estado Novo demolished between the 1930s and 1960s. It records for posterity the *fado novo*'s rejection of the Estado Novo's will, and thus serves as an apology to those who will accuse the national song of fostering the regime's values.

Every April, the Procession of Nossa Senhora da Saúde reminds Lisboners of the Mouraria that the Estado Novo did not demolish. And perhaps for years to come, when the Virgin passes through Largo da Guia in her litter, Lisboners will remember Gabriel de Oliveira's Rosa Maria, and her reverence of Mouraria tradition:

Tudo se ajoelha e reza
Até a Rosa Maria
Como que petrificada
Em ferverosa oração
É tal a sua atitude
Que a Rosa já desfolhada
Da Rua do Capelão
Parece que tem virtude.

[Everyone kneels and prays
Even Rosa Maria
As if petrified
In fervent prayer
Such is her attitude
That the deflowered rose
From Rua do Capelão
Seems virtuous.]

In his play and novel, Júlio Dantas renders a Mouraria that is, at once, holy and sordid. While his nineteenth-century Mouraria is set principally in and around the brothels of Ruas do Capelão and da

Amendoeira, the Catholic Church—always a presence in a quarter so close to the walled, medieval city center—haunts his work to remind the audience / reader of the morally ambivalent Mouraria. In this whorish yet devoutly Christian neighborhood, Dantas's Maria Severa represents an archetype of the nineteenth-century *fadista:* a figure lodged between sin and piety. Dantas's Severa simultaneously evokes our disdain and our compassion, for she is merely a victim of the Fado, a tenant of the Mouraria.

Dantas's portayal of the sympathetic whore who, despite her inevitably sordid life redeems herself through an intangible virtue, has become a mainstay of Fados set in the Mouraria, and furthermore, has served as a mold for the characterization of the nineteenth-century Mouraria *fadista* / prostitute. We observe Gabriel de Oliveira's Rosa Maria, from his Fado, "Há Festa na Mouraria," as an avatar of Maria Severa. Rosa Maria has lived a *fadista*'s life in the sad quarter, yet she is redeemed when she is overcome with religious devotion during the Procession of Nossa Senhora da Saúde.

Oliveira's Rosa Maria reappears in the *fado novo* of the 1930s to 1970s—like Maria Severa—as a vestige of the nineteenth-century Mouraria that is disappearing quickly. Rosa Maria's association with the Church of Nossa Senhora da Saúde, the last remnant of pre-Republican architecture in the Baixa Mouraria, calls our attention to the Mouraria that must be saved from the "Salvação Barreto" demolitions. After the virtual erasing of the aristocratic Mouraria, in the demolition of the Palace and Arch of the Marquis of Alegrete, the historical Mouraria that remains, and must remain, is characterized by its moral ambivalence. Thus the Church of Nossa Senhora da Saúde and Rosa Maria represent the character of the pre-Republican Mouraria as it confronts the sterile disaster of the Estado Novo's progress.

Conclusion: Good-bye, Mouraria

> Up until Amália Rodrigues appeared, the idolatry of Severa, the mythic ancestor of the Fado, had not been challenged.
>
> —António Osório

IN 1996, TERESA CASTRO D'AIRE ASKED SEVERAL *FADISTAS* IF THERE was a difference between Severa's Fado and the twentieth-century Fado. Carlos do Carmo responded that today's *fados novos* reflected changes in the Portuguese way of life, a consequence of social reform. He added, "Lisbon, the city that more than any other has been sung about in the Fado, in 1996 is not the same city that it was in 1936."[1]

Indeed Lisbon is not the same city that it was in the 1930s when the Estado Novo began its demolition projects that would change the architectural harmony of the capital by destroying part of its historical riverside. Nor is it the same city that it was at the turn of the century when Júlio Dantas wrote *A Severa,* as Portugal prepared for its Republican revolution. And certainly, the city has changed since the 1840s when Maria Severa sang her Fados in the Bairro Alto and the Mouraria.

Maria Severa would not recognize today's Baixa Mouraria. Surely, she would find her small home at 36 Rua do Capelão, where a cobblestone marker indicates one of the few remaining significant features of the devastated quarter.[2] Severa might recognize Largo da Guia, and even Rua da Amendoeira, where she and Barbuda had lived. But once she left the *fadista* quarter to the east of Rua da Mouraria, she would encounter a new city that represented something between repentant nostalgia and failed modernization.

Largo de Martim Moniz, the residential and commercial center of the Mouraria until the 1930s, is now a rotunda. The park, with its fountains and marble sidewalks, is better suited for the area than the macadamized parking lot that used to be there. Nevertheless, the landscape is cold, flat, and bleak. It is hard to imagine that frigid hole as a once-bustling melee of seventeenth- through nineteenth-century houses in need of the CML's care. On that blighted spot can we even fathom the charming, Alfama-like, albeit hectic and labyrinthine urban planning inherited from the Moors? Can we imagine the Baixa Mouraria as anything but Lisbon's cancer?

The contrast between what could have happened and what has happened to Lisbon's riverside is most evident to us as we cross the capital's oldest hill. Since the 1990s, Alfama has been benefiting from the EBAHL's (Equipamentos dos Bairros Históricos de Lisboa) renovation projects. The CML threw out the Estado Novo's notion of progress at the expense of tradition to promote Old Lisbon to the tourist, and to conserve it for the Lisboner. The result is a beautiful, preserved, and inhabitable Alfama. Here, riverside traditions flourish. Saint Anthony's Feast, grilled sardines, and pots of sweet basil seduce the tourist and the occasional Lisboner, who, perhaps condescendingly, believe that here time has stood still. Even the Fado has come back to Alfama to reinvigorate old neighborhood rivalries with the Bairro Alto.

Certainly, the Mouraria has its traditions, and what remains makes the neighborhood one of the most authentic corners of Lisbon. But as we look at Alfama's successful renovation that honors its *fadista*, noble, and Christian roots, can we help but flinch and hear the Fado as it sings "Adeus, Mouraria"?:

Adeus, Mouraria
Adeus, tradição
Já vejo a cidade
Cantar com saudade
A tua canção
E as casas velhinhas
Feitas pedraria
Vão pelo caminho dizendo
"Adeus, Mouraria."[3]

[Good-bye, Mouraria
Good-bye, tradition
I see the city
Singing nostalgically
Your song
And the little old houses

Turned to rubble
Drift down the street saying
"Good-bye, Mouraria."]

And as a new generation comes back to the Fado, does the farewell become more poignant or irrelevant?

Recently, I went to the Marialvas salon in Newark, New Jersey. I needed a haircut, and I could not resist a barbershop named after Dantas's archetypal character. As the stylist turned my swivel chair toward the mirror so that I could approve of my crew cut, I saw, beside my reflection, the stripes of the barber's pole. I remembered, for a brief instant, Mouraria *fadista*, Mariza's concert that I had seen in Boston a few years earlier. Mariza alluded to the legend of Maria Severa, as an introduction to her version of Gabriel de Oliveira's "Há Festa na Mouraria."[4] In a shy yet coquettish gesture, Mariza lifted the hem of her skirt to her knee to reveal black-and-white striped stockings identical to those worn by Dina Teresa in her role as Severa in Leitão de Barros's film, *A Severa;* the same stockings worn by Adelaide da Facada in José Malhoa's emblematic painting; the very hosiery of the caricatured Mouraria *fadistas*/prostitutes of Stuart Carvalhais's iconic cartoons. More than a century after Dantas created his folkloric avatar of the Mouraria *fadista*, and over a century and a half after Sousa do Casacão recorded in verse the impact of Severa's death, the memory of the nineteenth-century Mouraria *fadista* persists for Portuguese popular culture, so much that it is being exported to Luso-American audiences of the twenty-first century.

Fadistas cry! Is Severa dead?

Notes

Preface

1. "A Marcha da Mouraria," J. F. de Brito/Raúl Ferrão.

2. The subway station used to be called Socorro, for the parish of the homonymous church.

3. Tavares Dias, *Lisboa Desaparecida*, 1:20–21.

4. Tavares Dias, *Lisboa Desaparecida*, 1:20, comments, "In the eleventh hour, the little chapel was spared, some say, because of Salazar's own religious devotion."

5. "O meu Bairro," Conde de Sobral/Joaquim Campos.

6. Tavares Dias's chapter, "Ai, Mouraria," from *Lisboa Desaparecida*, vol. 1, is exceptional. She outlines motivations for and reactions to the demolitions of the Mouraria, and shows before-and-after photographs of the demolition projects. Dejanirah Couto's *Histoire de Lisbonne* synthesizes Tavares Dias's research on the Mouraria.

Introduction

1. Tavares Dias, *Lisboa Desaparecida*, 1:19, signals the Estado Novo's euphemism of progress: "'Recuperation' is a term that the Estado Novo did not use because the dominant 'philology' of the time considered old [Lisbon] a succession of quarters 'condemned to progress.'" Duarte Pacheco (1900–43) served as mayor of Lisbon and Minister of Public Works between 1938 and his accidental death in 1943. In Garnier, *Salazar in Portugal: An Intimate Portrait*, 56, Salazar says of Pacheco: "When he decided that one spot in Lisbon should be modernized, without hesitation he would tear down the whole neighborhood." França, *Lisboa. Urbanismo e Arquitectura*, 105, 131; Between 1938 and 1940, urban developer, E. de Gröer, served as Pacheco's consultant (Ana Homem de Melo in Santana and Sucena, eds., *Dicionário da História de Lisboa*, 676). Keil Amaral, *Lisboa, uma Cidade em Transformação*, 121; João Guilherme Faria da Costa (1906–71) was hired by the CML as a part of an urban development team, including Francisco Keil Amaral and Inácio Peres Fernandes, to continue the development begun by Pacheco under the "Plano de Remodelação da Baixa" (1944), in José Manuel Pedreirinho in Santana and Sucena, eds. *Dicionário da História de Lisboa*, 319.

2. Keil Amaral, *Lisboa, uma Cidade em Transformação*, explains the political and practical motivations for the project to widen Rua da Palma and Avenida do Almirante Reis (103).

3. França, *Lisboa*, 117; Vieira da Silva, *Plano Director de 1967*, 23.

4. França, *Lisboa*, 120, 131.

5. Araújo, *Peregrinações*, 3:61.
6. David, ed., *The Conquest of Lisbon*, 124–29.
7. Araújo, *Peregrinações*, 3:76–77; Real Irmandade, eds., *Breve Notícia*, 12; Real Irmandade, *Estatutos*, 6.
8. Araújo, *Peregrinações*, 3:76.
9. Tavares Dias, *Lisboa Desaparecida*, 1:20, indicates such a lesson as a benefit of the "Salvação Barreto" demolitions.
10. Araújo, *Peregrinações*, 3:68.
11. Ibid., 71.
12. Let us examine the recent demolition (1997–2001) of Casal Ventoso, a neighborhood—although historically insignificant—as socially problematical as the nineteenth-century Mouraria. It is inconceivable that the ruins of the infamous slums plagued by drug trafficking might generate a fond or even ambivalent folkloric memory of Casal Ventoso.
13. Pinto de Carvalho, *História do Fado*, 69; Castilho, *Lisboa Antiga: Bairros Orientais*, 3:51.
14. Portela, *Salazarismo e Artes Plásticas*, 15. In my translation, I borrow the word "showpiece" from Holton, *Performing Folklore: Ranchos Folclóricos from Lisbon to Newark*, 30.
15. Ferro, *Salazar*, 89.
16. Vieira Nery, *Para uma História do Fado*, 220. The censoring of Amália Rodrigues's recording of "Fado de Peniche (Abandono)" (David Mourão-Ferreira/Alain Oulman) for subversive content is testimony of the critical limits imposed on the *fado novo*. In Pavão dos Santos, *Amália*, 151, Amália Rodrigues says: "I always thought that David Mourão-Ferreira's 'Abandono,' was a love song. I never thought about Peniche . . . The prisons never even crossed my mind. It is a Fado that, even today, everybody likes. And everybody interpreted it differently. A revolutionary thought that it was about Peniche, but most people in Portugal, who are not so privileged, who were not so aware, who were like I was, thought about love."
17. Garnier, *Salazar in Portugal: An Intimate Portrait*, 190.
18. Vieira Nery, *Para uma História do Fado*, 193.
19. Ibid., 193.
20. Fado lyricist, Mascarenhas Barreto, explores *saudade* as a leitmotif in Portuguese song in *Fado: A Canção Portuguesa* and *Fado: Origens Líricas e Motivação Poética*. More recently, Maria Luísa Guerra studies the relevance of *saudade* in relation to navigation and literature of the Age of the Discoveries in *Fado: Alma de um Povo*.
21. Castro d'Aire, *O Fado*, 18.
22. During Severa's lifetime, Francisco Inácio dos Santos Cruz examined prostitution in Madragoa, the Bairro Alto, and the Mouraria in his study, *Da Prostituição na Cidade de Lisboa* (1841).
23. Palmeirim, *Os Excêntricos do Meu Tempo*, 285–86, comments: "[Severa's celebrity] later was consecrated in a book, in the Fado in which her death was mourned, and which Mr. Theophilo Braga recovered in his *Cancioneiro Popular* in the section fated to perpetuate in print 'Fados and Songs from the Streets.' "
24. Pinto de Carvalho, *História do Fado*, 61.
25. Pimentel, *A Triste Canção do Sul*, 140.
26. While Pimentel blames the "Fado da Severa" for the cult of the Mouraria *fadista*, he recognizes Camilo Castelo Branco's contribution to Severa's legend.

27. Pinto de Carvalho, *História do Fado*, 62, believed that Severa had lived on Travessa do Poço da Cidade (Bairro Alto) in 1844 or 1845.

28. Eça de Queiroz mentions the Fado in *Os Maias* (1888) (400, 402, 507, 531, 575, 650–51, 697) and *A Ilustre Casa dos Ramires* (1894) (57, 255–56, 288). We may contrast the opinion of Eça's character, Ega, that there is nothing, in art, as beautiful as the Fado, with Eça's most famous pronouncement on the Mouraria Fado: "Athens produced sculpture, Rome made laws, Paris invented the revolution, Germany discovered mysticism. What did Lisbon create? The Fado . . . *Fatum* was a God on Mt. Olympus; in these neighborhoods, it is a comedy. There is an orchestra of Portuguese guitars and the stage is illuminated by cigars. The props include a stretcher. The final scene takes place in the hospital and in the morgue. The final curtain is a shroud" (*Os Maias* 650; "Lisboa," 1).

Chapter 1. *A Severa*

1. Pinto de Carvalho, *História do Fado*, 61.
2. Pimentel, *A Triste Canção do Sul*, 141.
3. Sucena, *Lisboa, o Fado e os Fadistas*, 22.
4. Pinto de Carvalho, *História do Fado*, 62.
5. Pimentel, *A Triste Canção do Sul*, 156.
6. Sucena, *Lisboa, o Fado e os Fadistas*, 22.
7. "Maria Severa," José Galhardo/Raúl Ferrão.
8. Araújo, *Peregrinações*, 3:70.
9. Pinto de Carvalho, *História do Fado*, 62, believes that Severa was born in Madragoa. Pimentel, *A Triste Canção do Sul*, 144, explains that, according to Bulhão Pato—who told Urbano de Castro—Severa was a nickname (that alluded to her father's first name) that would become her *nome de guerre*. Severa's mother was known as Barbuda because she had facial hair.
10. In Dantas's novel, Barbuda/Cesária is the Count of Marialva's lover before he becomes Severa's lover. Severa's house at 36 Rua do Capelão exists today as the Mouraria's only tourist attraction.
11. Dantas's Barbuda/Cesária is based loosely on Severa's mother, Ana Gertrudes, and the late nineteenth-century *fadista*, Cesária, known as a Mulher da Alcântara. Sucena, *Lisboa, o Fado e os Fadistas*, 40, informs us that the character of Cesária in the operetta *Mouraria* (1926), by Lino Ferreira, Silva Tavares, Lope Lauer, and with music by Filipe Duarte, was inspired by Dantas's Cesária and the prostitute from Alcântara. Dantas's Barbuda/Cesária arrives in the Mouraria, having fled from a gypsy caravan in the Alentejo. Pinto de Carvalho, *História do Fado*, 62; Pimentel, *A Triste Canção do Sul*, 143; and Queriol, "Recordações da Minha Mocidade," 1, refute Severa's Gypsy heritage. Araújo, *Peregrinações*, 3:70, perhaps influenced by Dantas's and Leitão de Barros's creations, believed that Severa had come to Lisbon with a horde of gypsies. Because Barbuda lived in a tavern in Madragoa in 1820, we may assume that (like most inhabitants of that neighborhood) she was from Ovar or Estarreja. Dantas's Barbuda/Cesária does not love Severa, however, she is compelled by a maternal instinct to protect her daughter, especially from her likely fate of prostitution. When Dantas's Severa discovers the Fado and subsequently loses her virginity, Barbuda/

Cesária is devastated. Pimentel, *A Triste Canção do Sul*, 142, however, believed that Barbuda lacked maternal compassion and that it was she who prostituted Severa.

12. Pinto de Carvalho, *História do Fado*, 102, collected these verses, later variants of Sousa do Casacão's "Fado da Severa" (1848), from the oral tradition.

13. Pinto de Carvalho, *História do Fado*, 61; Pimentel, *A Triste Canção do Sul*, 144.

14. Queriol's article appeared in *O Popular* on April 7, 1901 shortly after the January 25, 1901 debut of *A Severa: Peça em Quatro Actos*, as a vindication of the Count of Vimioso's character. Raimundo António Bulhão de Pato, also a contemporary of Severa, responded to support Queriol's apologia of the Count. Queriol's portrait confirms some of the gentler characteristics of Dantas's Severa.

15. When Palmeirim, *Os Excêntricos do Meu Tempo*, 292, visits Severa in the Bairro Alto he calls her a woman who lacked "two of the principal feminine attributes—modesty and timidity." When Queriol, "Recordações da Minha Mocidade," 1, meets Severa at the Count of Vimioso's Palace in Campo Grande, he characterizes the *fadista* as "subservient and quite aware that she is not the lady of the house." He credits Severa's shyness to her discomfort among nobility.

16. Luís, *Fado, Mulheres e Toiros*, 28; Osório, *A Mitologia Fadista*, 28–29.

17. Sousa e Costa, *Severa*, 112.

18. André Brun adapted Dantas's novel and play (*A Severa: Peça em Quatro Actos*, 7–8) as an operetta, with music by Filipe Duarte, in 1909. In the late 1920s and 1930s, Dantas's play, *A Severa: Peça em Quatro Actos*, appeared in other parts of Europe. It had been translated to Catalan by Ribera y Rovira, and later appeared, in Spanish, at the Teatro Roméa in Barcelona (translated by José Palacios and Eugenio López Aydillo). Louise Ey translated the drama to German in 1920. *A Severa* was adapted to Spanish musical theatre by Francisco Romero and Guillermo Fernández Shaw, with music by Rafaél Millán. After having appeared at the Teatro Apolo in Madrid, the musical adaptation appeared at the Coliseu de Lisboa in 1931.

19. Sucena, *Lisboa, o Fado e os Fadistas*, 359–60, reports that Malhoa's painting was exhibited for the first time at the Sociedade Nacional de Belas-Artes in 1917. *O Fado* is on display at the Museu da Cidade in Campo Grande.

20. "Cinco Quinas," Fernando Farinha.

21. "Fado Malhoa," José Galhardo/Frederico Valério. "Fado Malhoa" profits from Dantas's proposal of the Fado as the national song in its verse: "Pintou numa tela com arte e com vida / A trova mais bela da terra mais querida" [He painted artfully on a canvas and brought to life / The most beautiful song from the most beloved land], and again in the verse: "Subiu a um quarto onde viu / À luz de petróleo / E fez o mais português/ Dos quadros a óleo" [He went up to a room / Lit by gas lamps / And created the most Portuguese / Of all oil paintings].

22. Macedo de Sousa, *Humores ao Fado e à Guitarra*, 28.

23. Ibid., 39.

24. Ibid., 50.

25. França, *A Arte em Portugal no Século XX*, 2:284.

26. Ângela Pinto debuted in the role of Maria Severa in 1901 at the Teatro D. Amélia. Bénard da Costa, *Histórias do Cinema*, 50, remarks that when Leitão de Barros began working on the idea for his adaptation of *A Severa* in 1918, he considered casting Pinto. However, he decided that the new medium needed a new face, so he chose the young chorus girl, Dina Teresa Moreira. The performances of *A Severa: Peça em*

Quatro Actos starring Amália Rodrigues (Teatro Monumental 1955) and Lena Coelho (Teatro Maria Matos 1990) have perpetuated Dantas's image of the Mouraria well into the end of the twentieth century. In Pavão dos Santos, *Amália*, 115, Amália says of her role as Severa: "Since there was nobody to direct me, I went around rehearsing the part with my legs spread, like Severa, but I didn't know what I was doing. That whole business of a brassy woman, with hairy arms and fire in her eyes had nothing to do with me. After a few days, I wanted to quit . . . I decided to stay and *fazer uma amaliazada* [do the Amália act]. I made Severa come to me. I had no idea what Severa was like!" Pavão dos Santos, *Amália*, 292; Augusto Fraga directed a series of short films, based on Amália's Fados, including "Fado Malhoa," in Madrid in the summer of 1947 (296). The video clip appeared with feature films in Portuguese movie theaters in 1948 and 1949. The video clip appears in Bruno de Almeida's 1995 documentary, *Amália: Uma Estranha Forma de Vida*, based on Pavão dos Santos's interviews with Rodrigues.

27. Palmeirim, *Os Excêntricos do Meu Tempo*, 288.

28. Ibid.

29. Dantas, *A Severa*, 217.

30. Macedo de Sousa, *Humores ao Fado e à Guitarra*, 30.

31. "Novo Fado da Severa (Rua do Capelão)," Júlio Dantas/Frederico de Freitas.

32. Araújo, *Legendas*, 134.

33. "Novo Fado da Severa (Rua do Capelão)" was recorded later by Amália Rodrigues, Fernanda Maria, and Alexandra.

34. Sucena, *Lisboa, o Fado e os Fadistas*, 124.

35. Macedo de Sousa, *Humores ao Fado e à Guitarra*, 44, remarks that a 1927 law demands that Fado houses and singers carry professional licenses. Sucena, *Lisboa, o Fado e os Fadistas*, 213–14, signals the professionalization of the *fadista* and the lyricist of the 1930s to 1950s as the Fado's golden age. Furthermore, he attributes the launching of Rádio Colonial in the 1930s with having brought the Fado to a national audience. For more on the evolution of Portuguese radio, see Estrela, *A Publicidade no Estado Novo*, vol 1. For more on the post-1927 professionalization of the *fadista*, see Colvin, "Perdigão Queiroga's Film."

36. Araújo, *Legendas*, 133. Bénard da Costa, *Histórias do Cinema*, 82, n. 82, explains that, in 1944, the Secretariado de Propaganda Nacional changed its name to the Secretariado Nacional de Informação, because after World War II, the term "propaganda" had negative connotations. Paulo, *Estado Novo e Propaganda*, 79, comments that "the new name [SNI] camouflages the development of an apparatus of propaganda, which became significantly more repressive and sophisticated than the modest SPN": translation in Holton, *Performing Folklore*, 237, n. 3.

37. In Machado, *Ídolos do Fado*, 1, Artur Inês says in the preface: "Taking the Fado away from the masses would be like closing off their only air valve in the narrow limits of their aesthetic and artistic tastes."

38. Bénard da Costa, *Histórias do Cinema*, 67.

39. Ibid., 67–68.

40. França, *Lisboa*, 112. The CML's 70-minute, silent documentary, *Melhoramentos Citadinos* (1931) tracks some of Lisbon's projects for urban expansion between 1926 and 1930, including the paving of Avenida da Índia and Avenida de Belém, and the controversy over the construction of Parque Eduardo VII. The film addresses the

issue of necessary projected demolitions for the sake of safety and hygiene in Alfama and Ribeira Velha. The documentary's optimistic title reflects both CML and public sentiment about urban development in Lisbon in the years preceding Duarte Pacheco's term as mayor and Minister of Public Works.

41. Nuno Teotónio Pereira in Santana and Sucena eds., *Dicionário da História de Lisboa*, 777.

42. França, *Lisboa*, 109.

43. Santana and Sucena, eds., *Dicionário da História de Lisboa*, 56–57; Câmara Municipal de Lisboa (CML), *A Urbanização do Sítio de Alvalade*, 20.

44. "Antigamente," Joaquim Proença/Frederico de Brito: "A Mouraria / Mãe do fado doutras eras / Que foi ninho de severas / Que foi bairro turbulento" [The Mouraria / Mother of the Fado of days gone by / It was once the nest of severas / It was once a chaotic quarter]. Araújo, *Legendas*, 132, mentions the Rua do Capelão of the " 'severas' who made their nest there."

45. Araújo, *Peregrinações*, 3:70.

46. "Já Não Vou à Mouraria," Ferrer Trindade/António José.

47. "Ai, Mouraria," Amadeu de Vale/Frederico Valério.

48. Macedo de Sousa, *Humores ao Fado e à Guitarra*, 60.

49. Dantas, *A Severa: Peça em Quatro Actos*, 70.

50. Ibid., 70.

51. Arroio, *O Canto Coral*, 58.

52. Ibid.

53. Lopes Vieira, *Em Demanda do Graal*, 352.

54. Sousa, *O Fado e os seus Censores*, 42.

55. "Ah, Fado dum Ladrão," Óscar Gusmão Martins/Carlos dos Santos.

56. In Dantas's novel, after having attended an opera at the Dona Amélia Theatre, the Count of Marialva and his friends go to the Bairro Alto to hear Severa sing.

57. "Anda Comigo," João Nobre.

58. "Tia Macheta," Manuel Soares/Linhares Barboso.

59. Here, the Fado alludes to Dantas's delicate novelistic character, the Marchioness of Ceide, whom the Count of Marialva rebuffs in favor of Severa.

60. Pimentel, *A Triste Canção do Sul*, 86.

61. Dantas, *A Severa: Peça em Quatro Actos*, 148.

62. Pimentel, *A Triste Canção do Sul*, 155.

63. Ibid., 155–56.

64. Pinto de Carvalho, *História do Fado*, 78–79.

65. Pimentel, *A Triste Canção do Sul*, 155.

66. Ibid., 87–88.

67. Dantas, *A Severa*, 292.

68. Dantas, *A Severa: Peça em Quatro Actos*, 57. Sousa e Costa, *Severa*, 69, reports that while she was sick in 1846, Severa told Joaquim António da Silva: "Joaquim, let me follow my fate. . . . I can't live without the guitars, the bullfights, the happy suppers and the parting of the horse-drawn carriages! . . . Leave me alone; leave me alone, Joaquim! . . . Go your own way. I'm not the woman for you—get away from me for I can't make anyone happy!"

69. Dantas, *A Severa: Peça em Quatro Actos*, 174–79.

70. Ibid., 196.

Chapter 2. Severa's Death

1. Sucena (*Lisboa, o Fado e os Fadistas,* 23) and Morais (*Fado e Tauromaquia no Século XIX,* 169–70) explain that in 1900, when Júlio Dantas was preparing his stage production of *A Severa: Peça em Quatro Actos* for its debut at Teatro D. Amélia (S. Luís), Hintze Ribeiro, acting on behalf of the Count of Vimioso's family, asked the author to omit the nobleman's character from the play. Dantas gave the character the apocryphal name of the Count of Marialva. *Marialvismo* refers to the rules of horseback riding established by D. Pedro de Alcântara de Meneses, Marquis of Marialva (1713–99) in his book *Método de Equitação.* The term *marialva* has come to mean a talented rider, yet connotes a type of nobleman or bourgeois who dresses extravagantly, fights bulls, and seduces—and often mistreats—women. When Dantas obscured Vimioso's name by calling his protagonist the Count of Marialva, he honored the nobleman as an equestrian and slandered him as a gentleman. For more on *marialvismo* in the popular, social context see José Cardoso Pires, *Cartilha do Marialva;* as a key to understanding social libertinism in nineteenth-century Portugal, see Miguel Vale de Almeida, "*Marialvismo:* A Moral Discourse in the Portuguese Transition to Modernity."

2. Pinto de Carvalho, *História do Fado,* 79.

3. Sousa e Costa, *Severa,* 47.

4. Pimentel, *A Triste Canção do Sul,* 154.

5. Sucena, *Lisboa, o Fado e os Fadistas,* 34.

6. Osório, *A Mitologia Fadista,* 40.

7. Dantas, *A Severa,* 236.

8. "Quando a Severa Morreu," António Vilar da Costa/Júlio Proença.

9. "Fado da Severa," Sousa do Casacão (João José de Sousa).

10. Pinto de Carvalho, *História do Fado,* 104, collected these verses from oral tradition. In Dantas, *A Severa,* 237, a *fadista* sings from the "Fado da Severa": "Chorai, fadistas chorai / Que a Severa já morreu" [Cry, *fadistas* cry / for Severa is dead] during Severa's funeral procession. In Dantas, *A Severa: Peça em Quatro Actos,* a chorus of *fadistas* sings the verse when Severa collapses (200). Dantas, however, must resort to ellipsis to avoid anachronism, as the previous lines of the "Fado da Severa" would read: "Hoje mesmo faz um ano / Que a Severa faleceu" [A year ago today / Severa died].

11. Macedo de Sousa, *Humores ao Fado e à Guitarra,* 48.

12. "Chorai, Fadistas, Chorai," António Rocha/Fado Menor.

13. Dantas, *A Severa,* 236.

14. Dantas, *A Severa: Peça em Quatro Actos,* 70.

15. Ibid., 110.

16. "Novo Fado da Severa (Rua do Capelão)," Júlio Dantas/Frederico de Freitas.

17. Pinto de Carvalho, *História do Fado,* 69, compares Severa to her contemporary, Marie Duplessis, inspiration for Alexandre Dumas's (fils) Marguerite Gautier, in his novel *La Dame aux Camélias* (1848).

18. I saw Severa's death certificate at the L94 exhibit, *Fado: Vozes e Sombras* at the Museu de Etnologia, Belém in 1994. For more on the promotion and organization of the L94 exhibit, see Holton, "Bearing Material Witness to Musical Sound" and *Performing Folklore.* For more on the Fado exhibit, see Pais de Brito, *Fado: Vozes e Sombras.*

19. Sousa e Costa, *Severa*, 142, bases his argument on the erroneous assumption that all stroke victims lose their ability to speak.

20. Ibid., 67.

21. Ibid., 141.

22. "Canção da Desgraçada" ("Fado Choradinho"), César das Neves/A. Branco.

23. Sousa e Costa, *Severa*, 141; Dantas, *A Severa: Peça em Quatro Actos*, 119.

24. Macedo de Sousa, *Humores ao Fado e à Guitarra*, 28.

25. Halpern, *O Futuro da Saudade: O Novo Fado e os Novos Fadistas*, 14, classifies the generation of young *fadistas* of the 1990s and 2000s as *novos fadistas*. However, in his preface to Halpern's book, Vieira Nery cautions: "Maria Severa's Fado, in the dawn of the 1840s, certainly was a 'new Fado' compared to the dance that was sung on the docks and in the noble salons of Rio de Janeiro," 2–3.

26. Dantas, *A Severa*, 236.

27. Estrela, *A Publicidade no Estado Novo*, 1:86–87, signals that the first Portuguese radio station, Rádio Hertz, appears in 1914. In 1923, ORSEC broadcasts in Porto; in 1924, Rádio Lisboa/Rádio Colonial is founded in the capital. In 1925, CT1AA, CT1DH, and Rádio Condes appear in Lisbon, and Ideal Rádio and Rádio Porto in the *cidade invicta*. In 1928, Rádio Clube da Costa do Sol (Rádio Português) and Rádio Acordeon broadcast in Lisbon, followed in 1929 by Rádio Sonora (Voz de Lisboa) and Rádio Motorola. The 1933 appearance of the Emissora Nacional, the voice of the Estado Novo, would play a significant role in the regular diffusion of the *fado novo*. Sucena, *Lisboa, o Fado e os Fadistas*, 214, indicates that between 1937 and 1959, Rádio Clube Português hosted live broadcasts of Fado.

28. Porto, *O Comércio do Porto*, 13; Sucena, *Lisboa, o Fado e os Fadistas*, 354.

29. Eça de Queiroz, *Os Maias*, 650.

30. Gallop, *Cantares do Povo Português*, 17.

31. "Mataram a Mouraria," José Mariano/Manuel Maria Rodrigues.

32. "Fado, Não Sei Quem És," Silva Tavares/Frederico de Freitas.

33. See Colvin, "Perdigão Queiroga's Film."

34. Bénard da Costa, *Histórias do Cinema*, 70.

35. "Fadista Louco," Domingo Gonçalves Costa/Francisco Viana.

36. "Pobre Bairro," Júlio Proença.

37. "Anda o Fado n'Outras Bocas," Artur Ribeiro.

38. "Fado Loucura," Júlio de Sousa/Frederico de Brito. Variations of "Fado Loucura" have echoed Sousa do Casacão's refrain from the "Fado da Severa":

> "Chorai, chorai, guitarras da minha terra / O vosso pranto encerra / A minha vida amargurada / E se é loucura / Amar-te desta maneira / Quer eu queira quer não queira / Não posso amar-te calada"

> [Cry, cry, guitars of my land / Your plaint sums up / My bitter life / And if it is madness / To love you so / Whether I want to or not / I cannot love you in silence];

> "Chorai, chorai, poetas do meu país / Troncos da mesma raíz / Da vida que nos juntou / E se vocês / Não estivessem ao meu lado / Então não havia fado / Nem fadistas como eu sou"

> [Cry, cry, poets of my land / Trunks sprouted from the same root / Of a life that brought us together / And if you were not beside me / There would not be Fado / Or *fadistas* like I am];

and

> "Chorai, chorai, guitarras da minha terra / Que o vosso pranto encerra / As mágoas do passado / O mundo a rir / A rir às gargalhadas / Não tem dó das desgraçadas / Que morrem cantando o fado"
>
> [Cry, cry, guitars of my land / Your plaint sums up / The pain of the past / A laughing world / Laughing heartily / Feels no pity for the disgraced / Who die while singing the Fado].

Chapter 3. The Reconstruction of a Mouraria

1. França, *Lisboa*, 98.
2. Araújo, *Peregrinações*, 3:59–60.
3. Ibid., 60.
4. França, *Lisboa*, 108–9. Chantal, *A Vida Quotidiana em Portugal ao Tempo do Terramoto*, 244, refers to the Mouraria and the Bairro Alto in her description of Lisbon's poor sanitation in the years following the 1755 earthquake: "The streets were cluttered with dead animals, excrement and so many rotten scraps that it is quite surprising that more people did not get ill. The sun purified, the wind dispersed the puddles. In the summer, the mud would dry up and turn into a fine, black dust that would permeate the window shades of houses and the leather curtains of carriage litters. One would have to change stockings two or three times a day." Santos Cruz, *Da Prostituição na Cidade de Lisboa*, 57, describes the filthy conditions of the homes of streetwalkers in the Mouraria, the Bairro Alto, the Cotovia, and Madragoa, and suggests that Portugal not tolerate such a class of prostitution, which he considers most responsible for the spreading of venereal diseases.
5. Queriol, "Recordações da Minha Mocidade," and Bulhão Pato, "Severa," wrote letters in protest of Júlio Dantas's characterization of the Count of Vimioso, whose literary avatar, the Count of Marialva, threatens Custódia with a knife. Stuart Carvalhais, "Ouvindo o Fado Histórico," satirizes the Romantic, yet macabre character of the nineteenth-century Fado in his cartoon: "This Fado is lovely, especially the part in which the girl is stabbed to death and marries the Count."
6. Maria Júlia Ferreira in Santana and Sucena, eds., *Dicionário da História de Lisboa*, 57, characterizes Faria da Costa's plans for the Alvalade neighborhood as "socio-spatial integration, blending different types of homes that corresponded to different social classes." *Fadista*, Nuno da Câmara Pereira in Castro d'Aire, *O Fado*, 3–4, speaks of the cultural exchange between *fadistas* and aristocrats in Lisbon, when remembering his ancestral home in the Pátio de D. Fradique in Alfama: "If we want to appreciate, and compare the poor man's hovel to the rich man's palace, we can confirm that on the narrow streets of old Lisbon the two existed side by side, therefore there has always been, by obligation, a certain conviviality between the nobility and the people. That is why the Fado made it into noble salons . . . After all, a phenomenon occurred here that was a sort of a social exchange, that ended up enriching both classes."
7. "O que Sobrou da Mouraria," Paulo Fonseca, César de Oliveira, and Rogério Bracinha/João Nobre.
8. Araújo, *Peregrinações*, 3:78–79.

9. Araújo, *Legendas*, 135.
10. Araújo, *Peregrinações*, 3:79.
11. Araújo, *Legendas*, 135.
12. Ibid., 135.
13. Male *fadistas* from the Mouraria seduce noble women in the Fados, "O Chico da Mouraria," Nuno de Aguiar; and "Biografia do Chico," J. F. Oliveira/Nobrega e Sousa.
14. Pinto de Carvalho, *História do Fado*, 76–77.
15. "Fado Sonho," Francisco Duarte Ferreira/José Marques; "Fado à Luz da Candeia," Óscar Gusmão/M. Caro.
16. Armando "Armandinho" Augusto Freire (1891–1946) was the Lisbon Fado's most famous Portuguese guitarist.
17. See Barreto, *Fado: Origens Líricas e Motivação Poética;* Pinto de Carvalho, *História do Fado;* Gallop, *Cantares do Povo Português;* Moita, *O Fado, Canção de Vencidos;* Osório, *A Mitologia Fadista;* Pimentel, *A Triste Canção do Sul;* Ramos Tinhorão, *Fado: Dança do Brasil, Cantar de Lisboa;* and Vieira Nery, *Para uma História do Fado,* for more on the disputed relationship between *modinhas, lunduns,* and the Fado.
18. Vieira Nery, *Para uma História do Fado*, 57–59.
19. Dantas, *A Severa*, 136–37.
20. Ibid., 113.
21. Osório, *A Mitologia Fadista*, 24.
22. Vieira Nery, *Para uma História do Fado*, 60.
23. Although the Fado's Portuguese origins have been debated, Rodney Gallop, *Cantares do Povo Português*, 20, calls the song "an absolutely authentic urban song."
24. Vieira Nery, *Para uma História do Fado*, 60–61, identifies Queriol's reference as the first evidence of class mixing between the inhabitants of the degraded popular neighborhoods and nobility within the same social spaces.
25. "Fado do Embuçado," Gabriel de Oliveira/José Marques. Rocha Peixoto, *Terra Portuguesa*, 17, remarks that since the first quarter of the nineteenth century, even royalty enjoyed the Fado, and that, as a prince, D. Miguel "vigorously played the Fado." Sucena, *Lisboa, o Fado e os Fadistas*, 152, tells us that D. Luis I, D. Maria Pia, D. Amélia, and Prince D. Afonso liked to listen to the Fado. He explains that the "Fado do Embuçado" may refer to the nocturnal escapades of D. Carlos I who learned to play the Portuguese guitar with João Maria dos Anjos.
26. "O Marquês de Linda-a-Velha," Carlos Conde/Manuel Maria.
27. Osório, *A Mitologia Fadista*, 51.
28. Ibid., 50–51.
29. Let us remember that Camilo Castelo Branco's *Noites de Insónia* (1874) and *Eusébio Macário* (1879) are contemporary to the concert at the Casino Lisbonense. The caricature of the Mouraria *fadista* appears in musical theatre between the 1850s and 1890s, when the song will become a mainstay of the genre well into the 1950s.
30. Pimentel, *A Triste Canção do Sul*, 185.
31. Osório, *A Mitologia Fadista*, 43.
32. Ibid., 43.
33. Machado, *Lisboa na Rua*, 136.
34. "Biografia do Fado," Frederico de Brito.
35. Palmeirim, *Os Excêntricos do meu Tempo*, 288.

36. Pinto de Carvalho, *História do Fado*, 79.
37. "Encontro com o Passado," Manuel Viegas.
38. Osório, *A Mitologia Fadista*, 119.
39. Ibid., 119.
40. "O Café de Camareiras," Gabriel de Oliveira/Alfredo Marceneiro. Sucena, *Lisboa, o Fado e os Fadistas*, 121, describes the *cafés de camareiras* of turn-of-the-century Lisbon: "In these [cafes-cum-whorehouses], illuminated by gas lamps, the women of the 'trade' served a black, muddy coffee, commonly known as '*carocha*' (*carioca?*), and they sang the Fado accompanied sometimes by Portuguese guitar, sometimes by piano . . . The last of the *cafés de camareiras*, Boémia—where as late as 1925/ 1926 the Fado, accompanied by piano, was the main attraction—turned into an unsuccessful dancehall that closed in the '50s." Vieira Nery, *Para uma História do Fado*, 180–81, explains that between 1910 and 1920 cafes and pubs where Fado was sung appeared in Lisbon. These cafes attracted a middle-class clientele who were not accustomed to attending Fado sessions in the bars and cafes of the popular neighborhoods.

Chapter 4. Church of Nossa Senhora da Saúde

1. "Maria Severa," José Galhardo/Raúl Ferrão.
2. "Quando a Severa Morreu," António Vilar da Costa/Júlio Proença.
3. "Maria da Cruz," Frederico Valério/Amadeu do Vale.
4. "Malmequer Pequenino," Ricardo Borges de Sousa.
5. "Na Capelinha da Guia," Manuel Bogalho/Joaquim Campos.
6. "Canção da Desgraçada" ("Fado Choradinho"), César das Neves/A. Branco.
7. Araújo, *Peregrinações*, 3:61.
8. "O meu Bairro," Conde de Sobral/Joaquim Campos.
9. Araújo, *Peregrinações*, 3:60.
10. Matos, *Lisboa Islâmica*, writes about the Islamic occupation of Lisbon, and the Christian quarter outside the city's walls.
11. Gabriel de Oliveira, also known as Gabriel Marujo, was born on Rua do Capelão. He was the author of the lyrics of "Ave Maria Fadista" (Frederico de Valério), "Fado do Embuçado" (José Marques), "Foi na Travessa da Palha" (Joaquim Frederico de Brito), "Igreja de Santo Estêvão" ("Fado Vitória"), "Inspiração" (Linhares Barbosa), "Maria Madalena" (Popular), "O Café de Camareiras" (Alfredo Marceneiro), and "Senhora do Monte" (Alfredo Marceneiro). I estimate that Oliveira wrote "Há Festa na Mouraria" between 1930 and 1933. Araújo, *Peregrinações*, 3:77, mentions that the song was still popular as late as 1937. In 1937 Beatriz Costa appeared in *Há Festa na Mouraria*, a musical review, with songs by Fernando Santos, at the Apolo Theatre in the Mouraria. We know that António Amargo's "Há Festa na Mouraria" was subsequent to Oliveira's, and that Amargo died in 1933. Oliveira died in 1948.
12. Araújo, *Peregrinações*, 3:77, tells us that the procession occurred every April 20 from 1570 until 1910. Maria do Carmo Cortez, in Santana and Sucena, eds., *Dicionário da História de Lisboa*, 874–75, informs us that the first procession occurred on April 20, 1570 and thereafter, every third Thursday in April until 1908.
13. Sucena, *Lisboa, o Fado e os Fadistas*, 317.
14. Pimentel, *A Triste Canção do Sul*, 58; Sucena, *Lisboa, o Fado e os Fadistas*, 121.

15. Pinto de Carvalho, *História do Fado*, 75–76, describes Rua da Amendoeira in the nineteenth century: "In 1832, the ruckus and the fighting on Rua da Amendoeira was out of hand. Not a day went by when that substantial meal [of violence] wasn't served up to fans of the genre."

16. Pinto de Carvalho, *História do Fado*, gives brief biographies of these Mouraria prostitutes.

17. "Há Festa na Mouraria," António Amargo/Alfredo Marceneiro. Oliveira's Fado adapts the medieval Galician-Portuguese lyrical tradition of *leixa-pren* [give and take]. Each verse of the first stanza of the Fado is repeated in order in the last line of the subsequent stanza. However, Amargo's Fado makes use of *leixa-pren* by ending each stanza with a verse from the first stanza of Oliveira's "Há Festa na Mouraria."

18. "Fado Falado," Aníbal Nazaré/Nelson de Barros.

19. "O Zé Manel Viu a Rosa Maria," M. Paião/A. Damas.

20. "O Leilão da Casa da Mariquinhas," Linhares Barbosa/Fado Corrido.

21. "Já Sabem da Mariquinhas," Carlos Conde/Fado Mouraria.

22. "Chico Faia," José Marques/Manuel Oliveira Santos.

23. "Fui ao Baile," Amadeu do Vale/Fernando do Carvalho.

24. Chantal, *A Vida Quotidiana em Portugal ao Tempo do Terramoto*, 254–55. Santos Cruz, *Da Prostituição na Cidade de Lisboa*, informs us that prostitution was tolerated in Lisbon according to sessions of the Courts of Évora and Viana in 1481–82 (43, 164–69). An edict issued on December 25, 1608 further legitimized urban prostitution. Legal codes dating to December 31, 1836 and a public session on May 15, 1836, allowed prostitution in Lisbon, with the objective of monitoring and controlling syphilis. Santos Cruz divides the Lisbon prostitute into three groups: the clandestine type who meets her clients discreetly and charges a higher fee for her services; the prostitute who lives moderately well, either in a brothel or alone; and the streetwalker who is visited by soldiers, sailors, and household servants. We find the latter in the nineteenth-century Mouraria on Largo da Guia and Ruas do Capelão, da Amendoeira, and das Atafonas. Sucena, *Lisboa, o Fado e os Fadistas*, 39, tells us that bordellos were outlawed in Lisbon in 1962.

25. Pinto de Carvalho, *História do Fado*, 73, 62.

26. Sousa de Costa, *Severa*, 108; Pinto de Carvalho, *História do Fado*, 74.

27. Dantas, *A Severa*, 17.

28. Carvalho, *História do Fado*, 77.

29. Dantas, *A Severa*, 17.

30. Pimentel, *A Triste Canção do Sul*, 100.

31. Sucena, *Lisboa, o Fado e os Fadistas*, 317.

32. Chantal, *A Vida Quotidiana em Portugal ao Tempo do Terramoto*, 255.

33. Santos Cruz, *Da Prostituição na Cidade de Lisboa*, 94–95.

34. Pinto de Carvalho, *História do Fado*, 70–71.

35. Palmeirim, *Os Excêntricos do meu Tempo*, 288.

36. Vieira Nery, *Para uma História do Fado*, 67.

37. Ibid., Vieira Nery is commenting on the "Fado da Desgraçada," César das Neves/A. Branco: "E Deus, que tudo perdoa / E a Virgem Nossa Senhora / Hão-de ouvir a alma que implora / Salvação à pecadora" [And God, who forgives everything / And Our Lady, the Virgin / Must hear the soul that begs / For the sinner's salvation].

38. Sousa e Costa, *Severa*, 153.

39. Ibid.

40. Araújo, *Peregrinações*, 3:77.

41. Real Irmandade de Nossa Senhora da Saúde e de São Sebastião, *Estatutos; Breve Notícia.*

42. Real Irmandade de Nossa Senhora da Saúde e de São Sebastião, *Estatutos; Breve Notícia.* The procession reappeared from 1940 until 1974, when it disappeared until 1981.

43. Araújo, *Peregrinações*, 3:76, says of the Church of Nossa Senhora da Saúde: "It is rather naïve; it reminds us of a village chapel, doesn't it?"

44. My thanks to Rui Afonso Santos, Museu do Chiado, for having explained to me the importance of these churches to the Estado Novo.

45. "Há Festa na Mouraria" appears on Amália's albums, "Foi Deus" (1953), "Maldição" (1967), and "Encontro com Don Byas" (1973). The Fado appears on Mariza's album, "Fado em Mim" (2001), in which Oliveira's lyrics are attributed to António Amargo, following the mistake in the liner notes of Amália Rodrigues's 1973 album. In 1972, Carlos do Carmo adapted António Amargo's "Há Festa na Mouraria" to the music of J. Marques's "Fado Nocturno." Although Alfredo Marceneiro had made Amargo's version of the Fado famous, his character—played by Francisco Sobral—appeared in Filipe la Féria's musical *Amália*, singing Oliveira's "Há Festa na Mouraria." I saw la Féria's play twice in 2000, at Lisbon's Politeama Theater, on Rua das Portas de Santão Antão, where the audience cheered when it recognized Oliveira's Fado.

46. "Evocando o Passado," F. Carvalhinho/D. G. Costa.

47. "Senhora da Saúde," Francisco dos Santos/Joaquim Campos.

48. "Ronda da Saudade," Fernanda Maria.

49. "Antigamente," Joaquim Proença/Frederico de Brito; "Fado Pechincha," João Carmo de Noronha/Maria Teresa de Noronha; "O que Sobrou da Mouraria," Paulo Fonseca, César de Oliveira, and Rogério Bracinha/João Nobre.

50. Macedo de Sousa, *Humores ao Fado e à Guitarra*, 60, comments that "the Fado began to disappear, as did the means of deceiving censorship."

51. "A Casa da Mariquinhas," Silva Tavares/Alfredo Marceneiro.

52. Rua dos Canos disappeared in the demolitions of 1956.

Conclusion

1. Castro d'Aire, *O Fado*, 121.

2. Pinto de Carvalho, *História do Fado*, 68, identifies the house as 36 Rua do Capelão in 1903; Araújo, *Peregrinações*, 3:70, places it at 34 Rua do Capelão in 1938; Sucena, *Lisboa, o Fado e os Fadistas*, 25, says that when Severa lived there, the house's address was 35 Rua do Capelão.

3. "Adeus, Mouraria," Artur Ribeiro.

4. Mariza sang at the Berklee Performance Center in Boston on April 22, 2004.

Bibliography

Araújo, Norberto de. *Legendas de Lisboa.* Lisbon: SPN, 1943.

———. *Peregrinações em Lisboa.* 15 vols. Lisbon: Vega, 1992.

Arroio, António. *O Canto Coral e a sua Função Social.* Coimbra, Portugal: n.p., 1909.

Barreto, Mascarenhas. *Fado: A Canção Portuguesa.* Lisbon: n.p., 1959.

———. *Fado: Origens Líricas e Motivação Poética.* Lisbon: Aster, 1970.

Bénard da Costa, João. *Histórias do Cinema.* Lisbon: Imprensa Nacional–Casa da Moeda, 1991.

Braga, Teófilo. *Cancioneiro Popular.* Lisbon: Imprensa Nacional, 1894.

Brun, André. *A Severa: Ópera Cómica em Três Actos.* Oporto, Portugal: n.p., 1912.

Bulhão Pato, António Raimundo. "Severa." *O Popular*, April 8, 1901.

Câmara Municipal de Lisboa. *A Urbanização do Sítio de Alvalade.* Lisbon: CML, 1948.

Cardoso Pires, José. *Cartilha do Marialva.* Lisbon: Dom Quixote, 1989.

Castelo Branco, Camilo. *Eusébio Macário.* Lisbon: Círculo de Leitores, 1983.

———. *Noites de Insónia.* Lisbon: Círculo de Leitores, 1983.

Castilho, Júlio de. *Lisboa Antiga: Bairros Orientais*, 12 vols. Lisbon: n.p., 1939.

Castro d'Aire, Teresa. *O Fado.* Lisbon: Temas da Actualidade, 1996.

Chantal, Suzanne. *A Vida Quotidiana em Portugal ao Tempo do Terramoto.* Lisbon: Livros do Brasil, n.d.

Colvin, Michael. "Gabriel de Oliveira's 'Há Festa na Mouraria' and the *Fado Novo*'s Criticism of the Estado Novo's Demolition of the Baixa Mouraria." *Portuguese Studies* 20 (2004): 134–51.

———. "Perdigão Queiroga's Film, *Fado, História d'uma Cantadeira:* Construction and Deconstruction of the *Fado Novo.*" *Portuguese Literary and Cultural Studies* 18 (forthcoming).

———. "Sousa do Casacão's 'Fado da Severa' and Júlio Dantas's *A Severa:* The Genesis of National Folklore in the Death of a Mouraria *Fadista.*" *Portuguese Literary and Cultural Studies* 16 (forthcoming).

Costa, Beatriz. *Sem Papas na Língua.* Rio de Janeiro: Civilização Brasileira, 1975.

Couto, Dejanirah: *Histoire de Lisbonne.* Paris: Fayard, 2000.

Dantas, Júlio. *A Severa.* Oporto, Portugal: Porto Editora, 1973.

———. *A Severa: Peça em Quatro Actos.* Lisbon: Portugal-Brasil, 1931.

David, Charles Wendell, ed. *The Conquest of Lisbon/De Expugnatione Lyxbonensi.* New York: Columbia University Press, 2001.

Dumas (fils), Alexandre. *La Dame aux Camélias.* Oxford: Oxford University Press, 2000.

Eça de Queiroz, José Maria de. *A Ilustre Casa dos Ramires*. Mem Martins: Ulisseia, n.d.

———. "Lisboa." *Gazeta de Portugal*, October 13, 1867.

———. *Os Maias*. Lisbon: Livros do Brasil, n.d.

EPUL, eds. *Plano de Renovação Urbana de Martim Moniz*. Lisbon: EPUL, n.d.

Estrela, Rui. *A Publicidade no Estado Novo*, 2 vols. Lisbon: Simplesmente Comunicando, 2004.

Ferreira, Lino, et al. *Mouraria: Coplas da Opereta Popular em três Actos*. Lisbon: Tipografia Costa Sanches, n.d.

Ferro, António. *Salazar*. Lisbon: Empresa Nacional de Publicidade, 1933.

França, José-Augusto. *A Arte em Portugal no Século XX*. 2 vols. Lisbon: Bertrand, 1974.

———. *Lisboa. Urbanismo e Arquitectura*. Lisbon: Instituto de Cultura e Língua Portuguesa, 1980.

Gallop, Rodney. *Cantares do Povo Português*. Lisbon: Instituto para a Alta Cultura, 1937.

Garnier, Christine. *Salazar in Portugal: An Intimate Portrait*. New York: Farrar, Straus and Young, 1954.

Guerra, Maria Luísa. *Fado: Alma de um Povo*. Lisbon: Imprensa Nacional–Casa da Moeda, 2003.

Halpern, Manuel. *O Futuro da Saudade: O Novo Fado e os Novos Fadistas*. Lisbon: Dom Quixote, 2004.

Holton, Kimberly da Costa. "Bearing Material Witness to Musical Sound: Fado's L94 Museum Debut." *Luso-Brazilian Review* 39.2 (2002): 107–23.

———. *Performing Folklore: Ranchos Folclóricos from Lisbon to Newark*. Bloomington: Indiana University Press, 2005.

Keil Amaral, Francisco. *Lisboa, uma Cidade em Transformação*. Lisbon: Publicações Europa-América, 1969.

Kessel, Joseph. *Les amants du Tage*. Paris: Librairie Plon, 1968.

Lopes Vieira, Afonso. *Em Demanda do Graal*. Lisbon: SNI, 1946.

Luís, Pepe. *Fado, Mulheres e Toiros*. Lisbon: Livraria Francisco Franco, 1945.

Macedo de Sousa, Osvaldo, ed. *Humores ao Fado e à Guitarra*. Lisbon: EBAHL, E.M. / Casa do Fado e da Guitarra Portuguesa, 2000.

Machado, Alberto Victor. *Ídolos do Fado*. Lisbon: Tipografia Gonçalves, 1937.

Machado, Júlio César. *Lisboa na Rua*. Lisbon: Frenesi, 2002.

Mântua, Bento. *O Fado*. Lisbon: Bertrand, 1915.

Matos, José Luís de. *Lisboa Islâmica*. Lisbon: Instituto Camões, 1999.

Morais, António Manuel. *Fado e Tauromaquia no Século XIX*. Lisbon: Hugin, 2003.

Moita, Luís. *O Fado, Canção de Vencidos*. Lisbon: n.p., 1936.

Neves, César das and Gualdino Campos. *Cancioneiro de Músicas Populares*. Lisbon: n.p., 1939.

Osório, António. *A Mitologia Fadista*. Lisbon: Livros Horizonte, 1974.

Pais de Brito, Joaquim. *Fado: Vozes e Sombras*. Lisbon: L94 / Electa, 1994.

Palmeirim, Luís Augusto. *Os Excêntricos do meu Tempo*. Lisbon: M. Gomes, 1891.

Paulo, Heloísa. *Estado Novo e Propaganda em Portgal e no Brasil: O SPN/SNI e o DIP.* Coimbra, Portugal: Livraria Minerva, 1994.

Pavão dos Santos, Vítor. *Amália.* Lisbon: Contexto, 1987.

Pimentel, Alberto. *A Triste Canção do Sul.* Lisbon: Dom Quixote, 1985.

Pinto de Carvalho, José. *História do Fado.* Lisbon: Dom Quixote, 1992.

Portela, Artur. *Salazarismo e Artes Plásticas.* Lisbon: Instituto de Cultura e Língua Portuguesa, 1982.

Porto, António. *O Comércio do Porto,* October 15–16, 1984.

Queriol, Miguel. "Recordações da Minha Mocidade." *O Popular,* April 7, 1901.

Ramos Tinhorão, José. *Fado: Dança do Brasil, Cantar de Lisboa.* Lisbon: Caminho, 1994.

Real Irmandade de Nossa Senhora da Saúde e de São Sebsastião, eds. *Breve Notícia Histórica sobre a Irmandade e Procissão de Nossa Senhora da Saúde e de São Sebsastião.* Lisbon: Real Irmandade de Nossa Senhora da Saúde e de São Sebsastião, n.d.

———. *Estatutos da Real Irmandade de Nossa Senhora da Saúde e de São Sebsastião.* Lisbon: Real Irmandade de Nossa Senhora da Saúde e de São Sebsastião, 1992.

Rocha Peixoto, António Augusto da. *Terra Portuguesa/Crónicas Científicas.* Oporto, Portugal: n.p., 1897.

Roseiro, António. *Fados Canções: Compêndio de Cantigas.* Lisbon: Gráfica Povoense, 1994.

Santana, Francisco and Eduardo Sucena, eds. *Dicionário da História de Lisboa.* Lisbon: Carlos Quintas, 1994.

Santos Cruz, Francisco Inácio dos. *Da Prostituição na Cidade de Lisboa.* Oporto, Portugal: n.p., 1841.

Sousa, Avelino. *O Fado e os seus Censores.* Lisbon: n.p., 1912.

Sousa e Costa, Júlio de. *Severa.* Lisbon: Bertrand, 1936.

Sucena, Eduardo. *Lisboa, o Fado e os Fadistas.* Lisbon: Vega, 2002.

Tavares Dias, Marina. *Lisboa Desaparecida.* 8 vols. Lisbon: Quimera, 1998.

Vale de Almeida, Miguel. "*Marialvismo:* A Moral discourse in the Portuguese Transition to Modernity." *Série Antropologia* 184 (1995): 1–17.

Vieira da Silva, A. *Plano Director de 1967.* Lisbon: CML, 1967.

Vieira Nery, Rui. *Para uma História do Fado.* Lisbon: Público, 2004.

Index